Presences of Nature
Words and Images of the Lake District

Presences of Nature

Words and Images of the Lake District

Edited by Neil Hanson

Carlisle Museum & Art Gallery

PUBLISHED BY CARLISLE MUSEUM & ART GALLERY
© CARLISLE MUSEUM & ART GALLERY 1982
DESIGNED BY ANDREW BARRON
PRINTED IN GREAT BRITAIN BY BALDING & MANSELL, WISBECH

BRITISH LIBRARY CIP DATA
PRESENCES OF NATURE:
WORDS AND IMAGES OF THE LAKE DISTRICT
1. LAKE DISTRICT (ENGLAND) – DESCRIPTION AND TRAVEL
I. HANSON, NEIL
914.27'804858   D670.L1

ISBN 0 907852 00 9 SOFT COVER
ISBN 0 9502457 9 8 HARD COVER

COVER ILLUSTRATION
GRASMERE WITH RYDAL WATER & WINDERMERE FROM SILVER HOWE
ADRIAN BERG, WATERCOLOUR

PRESENCES OF NATURE IS PUBLISHED WITH
THE FINANCIAL ASSISTANCE OF THE CITY OF CARLISLE
AND THE ARTS COUNCIL OF GREAT BRITAIN

Ye Presences of Nature in the sky
Or on the earth! Ye visions of the hills!
And Souls of lonely places! can I think
A vulgar hope was yours when ye employed
Such ministry, when ye through many a year
Haunting me thus among my boyish sports,
On caves and trees, upon the woods and hills,
Impressed upon all forms the characters
Of danger or desire; and thus did make
The surface of the universal earth
With triumph and delight, and hope and fear,
Work like a sea?

WORDSWORTH, THE PRELUDE

Contents

Preface

The work of Wordsworth, Turner and a host of others, is testimony to the inspiration that artists and writers have found in the Lake District in the past.

Though the region is still most widely known for the Lakes and Mountains at its core, Cumbria, the modern amalgamation of Cumberland and Westmorland, also spans the Solway Firth, the industrial coastlands of West Cumbria, the Northern shores of Morecambe Bay, the lush farmland of the Eden valley, the bleak rolling fellsides, Hadrian's Wall and the twin 'capitals' of Carlisle and Kendal separated by the granite bulk of Shap.

Presences of Nature is the product of a decision to assemble a substantial body of new work reflecting the beauty and variety of this Cumbrian landscape, and the diversity of response it engenders in some of our finest contemporary artists, writers, photographers and craftsmen.

The contributors to Presences of Nature have sought out those particular places within this large and divergent region that speak most strongly to them, and their work covers Cumbria in all areas, in all seasons, in all weathers and in all moods. Some have spent their lives in the shadow of the Lakeland hills, others made their first visits to research and produce the work for this book. They are united by the quality of their work and by their willingness to respond to the challenge of this landscape, the quiet knowledge gained by a lifetime in a place balanced by the insights that a fresh eye can bring.

NEIL HANSON

Melvyn Bragg

Born in Wigton, Cumberland in 1939. He was educated locally and at
Oxford, where he read Modern History. Since then he has made his living
as a novelist and broadcaster.
His novels have been published to widespread acclaim, they include: *For
Want of a Nail*, *The Second Inheritance*, *The Hired Man*, *A Place in England*,
Autumn Manoeuvres, *A Christmas Child* and *Kingdom Come*. He is also the
author of *Speak for England*, an oral history of England since 1900.
Melvyn Bragg is also well known as an editor and presenter of television
programmes. He originated, presented and edited *Read All About It*. He
has contributed many features to *The Lively Arts* series and is at present
editing and presenting *The London Weekend Television South Bank Show*.
As a screenwriter, he has written films including *Isadora*,
The Music Lovers, *Jesus Christ Superstar*.
He is a Fellow of the Royal Society of Literature.

Cumbria

For most people, Cumbria is 'The Lake District' and indeed, for more than two hundred years, travellers, poets, visitors and residents have glowingly reviewed this spectacular landscape soaring peacefully above the sea of troubles in the North-West plain. For Cumbria is also Border Country, centuries of pillage and vengeance; and, along the coastal strip, a cicatrice of the once exuberant and brutal entrepreneurial Victorian heavy industry is proof to yet another place. Beauty, War and Mining – three massive pillars dominate the history and present face of Cumbria and yet in my opinion, nothing so characterises the area as the work-a-day farms, particularly the hill farms which bind together the heartland of the place with an extraordinary tenacity.

In a sense, to call it 'The Lake District' is to do an injustice to its finest feature – the hills, or fells as they are called locally. These hump-backed bare uplands are among the oldest mountain ranges in the world. For over 500 million years the geological fantasia which included vast volcanic eras, times of desert and ice, Olympean land shifts and furies of resettlement, formed and reformed this involuted landscape. The Lakes came later. They could go comparatively soon. Silt builds up ceaselessly. But the hills, you feel – and this is the essential element in the allure of Cumbria – will stretch into the future as far as they reach back into the past.

It is the complication and the varying proportions of the place within the human scale which makes it so singular. Coleridge was the first to point it out and since then all of us who have walked the place have consciously and unconsciously subscribed to the same insight. For it seems such a little spot, in a way. Runners run through it in a day and a night: Josh Naylor, the King of fell runners, manages to pound up twenty or thirty peaks in a few hours. Whizz along the valleys in a car and you can take in most of the big lakes between sun-up and opening time. You would miss a lot. For the only way to see it as it deserves to be seen is to amble, to follow the sheep tracks or the way drawn out by Wainwright whose hand-written guides are both folk-lore and functional. And as you amble, to pause; frequently. For the hills are so close packed, the lakes so different, the valleys so particular, that if you are at all sensitive to variety then the richness of it will seep into and then saturate your senses.

The weather too will rarely hold still for more than a few minutes and indeed, as Turner and other lesser artists show dramatically, it has the quality of being in several conditions at the same time: you can have sun direct on Derwentwater, cloud to the West on Catbells, a fuming storm beyond the tip of the lake in Borrowdale and over Watendlath in the East, silvery strokes of light as clear as the lines on a sun dial. The ambling itself can be easy – up Skiddaw or Gable, around Rydal or by Ullswater – but, once again, the variety can be sudden. For inside those quiet humps are steeps and screes which continue to claim victims every year. It is both docile and dramatic.

Just as the other side to the embossed intricacy of the apparently small place is the limitless grandeur you can feel high mounted on a fell looking over a sea of peaks, so the dark side of those easy walks is only a few feet from your safe path. Rock-climbing began in this district almost 150 years ago and still now the valleys ring to the peals of ironmongery as hard muscled young men from the Northern cities batten to the rock face and seek to pick out a saving hold.

It is a fortress this central massif, and inside its natural barriers are scattered the remains of conquerors and conquered. Although much smaller than Stonehenge, the stones at Castlerigg near Keswick have a much more lonely mystery about them. The circle stands in full view of dozens of hill tops, as plain as an arena built to serve the seven hills of Rome – but built for what purpose? The even earlier Bronze Age circles – of which, again, there are several, mostly down in the Ulverston area, again stand bare of explanation, mockingly secure, telling no stories of those who laboured to construct them. Up in the Langdales, though, at Pike O' Stickle, you can touch the first real entry point of man in this area: you can even, still, find the instrument with which he hacked his way into the history of the place – the slate axe, quarried here, refined with the sand on the coast, so sharp it can still fell a forest and so useful that it was used by Cumbrians at the Battle of Hastings, approximately six thousand years after it had been perfected on these crinkled volcanic hills.

The Romans came of course and their most lasting impression on the Lake District natural fortress was a fortress of their own – at the top of Hardknott pass, poised there on the heights like the imperial eagle itself ready to swoop down on the constantly discontented inhabitants. The Romans left no trace in language or place-name: the Britons who had been there before re-emerged after centuries of centurions to merge with the Norsemen in what seems a reasonably amicable marriage – one which bred the dialect and character of the district so resolutely that the paternity is still everywhere apparent.

Once again Cumbria was lucky: the Bewcastle Cross and the Gosforth Cross are quite superb examples of the arts of the Anglian and Norse periods and to decipher them is to decode a cultural portrait of those warrior-farmers. Castles from the Normans of course – who never, legend claims, overran the independent centre of Cumbria – but castles begun and rebuilt at Kendal, Cockermouth, Penrith, Egremont – all about the entrances to the place. Churches above all the Cistercian monasteries most richly remaining at Barrow in the blood sandstone which softens so much of the building and in its gaunt ruins still emits feelings of that godly and profitable life which captured the souls of the Cumbrian and brought cultivation to many an isolated valley.

It has been, in effect though, a place on its own since the Norsemen came with their language which became and remains our dialect. Go to the Horse Fair at Wigton, the Shepherd's Meet in Wasdale, the Hound Trials all over the countryside and you will hear words more easily understood by Norwegians. Most Cumbrian names, mine included, are Norse: the names of all the natural features from fell to stayn (stone) are Norse: and the hill farmers work the same dour land with the same independence so admired by Wordsworth of the old Norse statesmen at Hawkshead.

Wordsworth is everywhere. The particularities of his poetry graph out so many spots – the Yew Trees in Lorton Vale, Glaramara's caves, Ullswater's daffodils, Michael's sheepfold – that you can take a journey through the countryside which is also a journey through his poetry. But his magnificence in insisting, in his work, on the symbiotic relationship between mankind and nature gave nature itself a new dimension for thoughtful observers and since then both literature and life have been enhanced. Here around Dove Cottage in Grasmere, in Cockermouth where he was born, or in the enchanting village of Hawkshead where he gained an education in sense and sensibility, you can be present still at what was the first spinning of that revolutionary weave of poetry and philosophy.

At school I received three collections of Wordsworth's poems as prizes over the years. We know our loyalties in Cumbria. I was born a few miles to the North of the Lakes and at first the rim line of Northern Fells seemed like a vision, some secret Xanadu rather intimidating. School trips and choir trips in plush musty buses were the first infiltrations and there were crowded voyages up Ullswater and down Windermere trying not to be sea sick, group rambles with the A.Y.P.A. and later longer explorations on bike and on foot with the cosy Youth Hostels always open at 5 p.m. I left when I was twenty and returned about a decade later – to the Northern Fells where the plain villages and the lack of lakes provides no encouragement for the general visitor and much selfish but most agreeable relief for those of us who live there. It is there, now that I learn about a place I had taken so much for granted, read poets other than Wordsworth; go to see the hundreds of prints and paintings done of the place, make a date with the Sports Meetings and Shows famously at Ambleside and Grasmere, but even more entertainingly in the smaller villages where Cumberland and Westmorland wrestlers in long johns and embroidered bathing trunks engage in ancient grappling, where fell runners rip to the top of crags and cascade down like a slither of scree and the men with the hound dogs wait for the scent layers to come in from their ten mile circuit which the hounds will follow over fell and field as the bookies shout the odds.

Nearer to me though, in the early days, were the two other parts of Cumbria, one by birth – the industrial coast – the other by geography – Carlisle. The town in which I was born, Wigton, is in the magnetic field of Carlisle, a Border City and capital of a rich and richly fought over plain. While to the West, the mining towns of Maryport, Workington and Whitehaven were where my father's family worked in the pits.

The Castle has been cut off from Carlisle now by a road which is probably efficient but leaves that splendid pile as gasping for its element as a pike on a river bank. When the road from the gates led directly into the old city, soon to reach the medieval Cathedral and the equally old Town Hall, then the place had a real feeling of its past. Here Bonnie Prince Charlie got on his White Horse and entered the English city with his hundred pipers before him. In that castle Kings of England and Scotland were crowned and parliaments convened. Men were hanged there for war and forgery; the heads of its defenders have been stuck on the spikes on its walls; and ballads came along the high and low roads leading north to the old enemy. North past the wall, called after Hadrian, begun by Agricola a stupendous barrier of stone and ditch and castle thrown across the waist of Britain: even now, walking along the reconstituted monument flanked by countryside frozen in gentle waves like a painted sea, the power of that imperial gesture can be felt.

The mining towns have taken a beating and they show the signs of it. There was a time, towards the end of the nineteenth century when Whitehaven was one of the leading ports in the land, when Humphrey Davy came to West Cumberland to continue his work, when discoveries in steel making were made which promised eternal riches for this remote mineral riddled area. Coal shafts went out under the Solway, men from Cornwall's closing tin mines came to work the iron ore, the Irish came over as they have done for six thousand years, to work on the mainland they had split away from: the place was revved up and ready to go. It went down. But still in the grid precision squares of Whitehaven and the attractively solid streets of Maryport which hump over to the harbour which Lowry drew so lovingly, you know that there was a Time . . . Hard times now though, with the irony of Atomic Energy replacing the closed coal mines, the disused ore shafts, the perilous steel works.

The people in those coastal towns were largely drawn from the fells and still the same interests and sports hinge them together. Still the whippets and ferrets, the poachers and fishermen, the men with dogs and the men with guns step out of their backdoors into the powerful seduction of the hills and the lakes. And the area now sees itself clearly, wants to keep what is good. Volunteer wardens clean up the popular walks: the professionals mend the paths: us amateurs make our children stuff their crisp bags in their pockets. For a place so much used, it is in a remarkable state of neatness.

There is a fairy tale aspect – not for nothing did Beatrix Potter invent her characters up here – and, at the right time of year, the lakeland towns and villages have an unperturbed serenity which taunts progress. Yet the visitors themselves represent progress – since the early eighteenth century when the English upper middle classes took to their own backyard and the new turnpikes took their new coaches up into Defoe's 'dreadful and horrid' wilderness of the North West. Genteel terror was the first inducement to these parts and the

printmakers and reporters laid on the horrors with all the greasepaint of circus clowns. That, too, was a fairy tale: even Wordsworth's pantheism has its faery aspect – and the sites in Cumbria which any dutiful visitor must see – Sawrey, Dove Cottage, the Abbot Hall Museum at Kendal, the Brockhole centre on Windermere, they too have their rather unreal dimension. Like the over grand nineteenth century mansions on the Southern lakes, like the sometimes over-twee folksiness of the shops, there is something about the place which makes the unreal gesture seem appropriate: and so fantasy and folly seems set in.

Those who keep the place on the ground are the hill farmers. Around me in the hamlet in which I live are men and women whose constant and ever absorbing occupation is with the land, what it gives and what feeds off it. They know that the primal wilderness still exists: they plough it down every year. They know the basic fact of existence: the lambs freeze solid in the snow. They know the strength and weakness of their own lives – the markets and the weather test their knowledge and endurance every week. It is there in the hill farms, that the truest life of Cumbria goes on, among men whose daily work takes them to the tops where they see around them the shape 500 million years have made and know how hard it is to hold what they have.

28th October, 1981

Colour Plates

NORMAN ACKROYD
Coniston Rainbow

ADRIAN BERG
Windermere and Grasmere from Wansfell Pike

18

ADRIAN BERG
Buttermere and Crummock Water

SUSANNA BIRLEY & GEOFFREY KEY
Beehive form

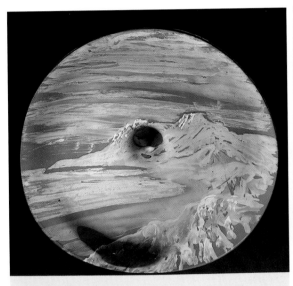 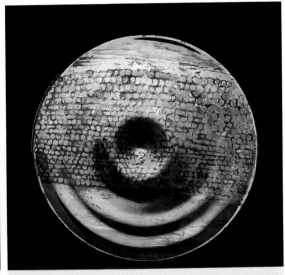

CHARLES BRAY
Landscape dish 1 & 2

21

ELIZABETH CLAY
Water Bowl, silver and yew wood

JENNY COWERN
Sky Felt 4

MIKE DAVIS
Landscape window

IAN GARDNER
Islands, Windermere

ANDY GOLDSWORTHY
Shallow trench edged with grass stalks, Brough

RICHARD HARRIS
Quarry structure, Grizedale Forest

JULIA HILLS
Winter and Spring

DAVID KEMP
The Chariot

FRANK NELSON
Cumbrian Sweet Dreams Machine

MELANIE SPROAT
Silver tantalum pomander

DONALD WILKINSON
Beside the lake, evening

Norman Ackroyd

Born in Leeds, England in 1938 and studied at the Leeds College of Art and the Royal College of Art which he left in 1964. His work has been exhibited widely in group exhibitions including the Bradford Print Biennale where he was a prize winner in 1972, and in others throughout Europe, and his paintings and prints are in many public and private collections throughout the world including the Victoria and Albert Museum, London and the Museum of Modern Art, New York.

Coniston Water

Wasdale Rain

Wasdale Screes

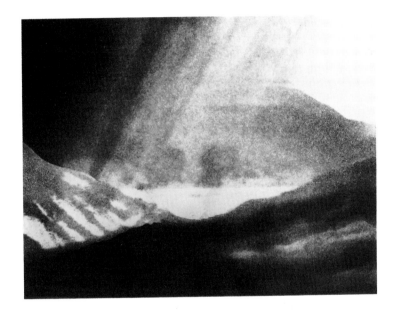

Windermere from Hardknott

Wastwater

Fleur Adcock

Born in New Zealand but has lived in England since 1963. In 1977/78 she was Arts Council Creative Writing Fellow at Charlotte Mason College, Ambleside, and in 1979/81 Northern Arts Fellow in Literature, living in Newcastle but with frequent visits to Cumbria. Her pamphlet *Below Loughrigg*, one of the outcomes of her year in Ambleside, was published by Bloodaxe Books in 1979; her most recent book-length collection of poems is *The Inner Harbour*, Oxford University Press 1979.

Maryport

This is a northern beach, and not playful.
All the buildings are for something, or were:
lighthouse, cargo sheds, tall stern houses
overseeing things from the hill behind.
The tide's half out. A drift of coal-chips
lines each ripple scored into the sand.
Seagulls are flakes of whitened ash
whirled against a smoky sky. No colour
except in the brick-red lumps of sandstone,
surprising boulders, blotched with khaki weed.

Not a fun place. But that is how the dog
sees it, waiting for a bunch of playmates.
And here they are: a man, a child, a woman
come to delight him from the only car
on this December Monday. Up he frolics,
making it clear that sticks are to be thrown.
No sticks: they strip a stem of leathery weed
and hurl that, with wildly varying actions,
in turns, over and over along the shore.
The wind's north-easterly. There could be snow.

The child sings to himself, plays games
with language, has invented a useful noun.
The man writes names on the sand. The woman
looks to them, and westward towards Ireland
and to the south, recalling other beaches
but learning the marks of this one by heart.
Sandpipers wheedle up from the rocks
where the dog goes hurtling; where, it is said,
there are plans for the construction of a marina.
The dog is happy; and will be happy then.

Binoculars

'What are you looking at?' 'Looking.'
High screed sides; possibly a raven,
he thought. Bracken a fuzz of rust
on the iron slopes of the fell
(off the edge of their map, nameless)
and the sky clean after rain.
At last he put the binoculars down,
drove on further to the north.

It was a good day in the end:
the cold lake lapping against pines,
and the square-built northern town idle
in sunlight. It seemed they had crossed borders.
Driving south became a return
to nests of trees in ornamental colours.
Leaving, he left her the binoculars
to watch her wrens and robins until spring.

Going out from Ambleside

1

He is lying on his back watching a kestrel,
his head on the turf, hands under his neck,
warm air washing over his face,
and the sky clear blue where the kestrel hovers.

A person comes with a thermometer.
He watches a ceiling for three minutes.
The person leaves. He watches the kestrel again,
his head pressed back among the harebells.

2

Today he will go over to Langdale
He springs lightly in his seven-league boots
around the side of Loughrigg
bouncing from rock to rock in the water-courses
evading slithery clumps of weed, skipping
like a sheep among the rushes
coursing along the curved path upward
through bracken, over turf to a knoll
and across it, around and on again
higher and higher, glowing with exaltation
up to where it all opens out.
That was easy. And it was just the beginning.

3

They bring him tea or soup.
He does not notice it. He is busy
identifying fungi in Skelghyll Wood,
comparing them with the pictures in his mind:
Purple Blewit, Yellow Prickle Fungus,
Puffball, Russula, two kinds of Boletus –
the right weather for them.
And what are these little pearly knobs
pressing up among the leaf-mould?
He treads carefully over damp grass,
patches of brilliant moss, pine-needles,
hoping for a Fly Agaric.

Scarlet catches his eye. But it was only
reddening leaves on a bramble.
And here's bracken, fully brown,
and acorns. It must be October.

4

What is this high wind coming,
leaves leaping from the trees to bite his face?
A storm. He should have noticed the signs.
But it doesn't matter. Ah, turn into it,
let the rain bite on the warm skin too.

5

Cold. Suddenly cold. Or hot.
A pain under his breastbone;
and his feet are bare. This is curious.

Someone comes with an injection.

6

They have brought Kurt Schwitters to see him,
a clumsy-looking man in a beret
asking for bits of stuff to make a collage.
Here, take my stamp-collection
and the letters my children wrote from school
and this photograph of my wife. She's dead now.
You are dead too, Kurt Schwitters.

7

This is a day for sailing, perhaps,
coming down from the fells to lake-level;
or for something gentler: for idling
with a fishing-line and listening to water;
or just for lying in a boat
on a summer evening in the lee of a shore
letting the wind steer, leaving the hull
to its own course, the waves to lap it along.

8

But where now suddenly? Dawn light,
peaks around him, shadowy and familiar,
tufts of mist over a tarn below.
Somehow he is higher than he intended;
and careless, giddy, running to the edge
and over it, straight down on splintery scree
leaning back on his boots, a ski-run
scattering chips of slate, a skid with no stopping
down through the brief mist and into the tarn.

9

Tomorrow perhaps he will think about Helvellyn . . .

Adrian Berg

Born in London in 1929 and educated at Caius College, Cambridge and
Trinity College, Dublin. He trained at St. Martin's, Chelsea and the
Royal College of Art. He received the Gold Medal at the Florence
Biennale in 1973, and the Lorne Scholarship in 1979–80.
He has had numerous one man and group exhibitions in Britain, Europe,
Japan and the USA. Public collections include Arts Council of
Great Britain, Northern Arts, Nuffield Foundation,
Tolly Cobbold and De Beers.

Skiddaw with Bassenthwaite Lake

Windermere from Jenkin Crag

Newlands with Derwent Water at the foot of Skiddaw from Latrigg

47

Wastwater, with Great Gable and the Screes

Charles Bray

Born in Salford, Lancs in 1922 and after war service in the Navy taught at various schools in Manchester and at Eden School, Carlisle until 1962. He lectured at Sunderland Polytechnic from 1962 to 1981, retiring as Principal Lecturer in Glass and Ceramics. Recent one man exhibitions include LYC Museum, Banks, Cumbria 1980 and Buddle Arts Centre, Wallsend 1981. Recent group exhibitions include Sunderland Art Gallery 1978; Gateshead 1979; *Northern Artists in Glass*, touring exhibition, Scottish Crafts Centre, Edinburgh 1980; *British Artists in Glass* touring exhibition also seen at the Prescote Gallery, Banbury, Mappin Gallery, Sheffield and Ceolfrith Gallery, Sunderland Arts Centre 1981.

Stack

Thomas A. Clark

Born in Greenock, Scotland in 1944 and now lives in the Cotswolds, where he is printer and publisher of Moschatel Press. His principal books are *A Still Life*, The Jargon Society 1977, *A Ruskin Sketchbook*, Coracle Press 1979, *Ways Through Bracken*, The Jargon Society 1980, and *Sixteen Sonnets*, Moschatel Press 1981.

Cat Leap Fall

All the walks lie
    along the line
Of a pronounced fault
    each of them returns
The walker
    to his starting point

Now proceed along
    the well-defined valley
Fringed with scars
    at a prominent tree turn
Look for an authentic crossing
    and persist

Walk slowly
    through the Happy Valley
And feel its calm
    a hollow vacated by
A glacier

The good path soon fades
    but go round
To find the small sinkhole
    though the day is calm
A clump of grass quivers
    as if shaken by a breeze

The trend is not
    towards the valley
But back
    into the heart
Into which trickles
    a small waterfall

This is the point
    of entry into

The underground system
    a system that has best
Resisted erosion
    along the shattered
Escarpment above

Delicate
    calcite traceries
Colonnades of
    massive stalagmites
Ceilings of slender
    opalescent stalactites
Floors and shelves littered
    with pearls and crystals

It is here
    in crannies of rock
May be found the purple
    saxifrage

Having reached a bed
    of impervious rock
These subterranean waters
    drain away or are forced
Out into daylight
    at risings or springs

Turn over the shoulder
    and ascend to where
This path breaks clear
    into open country
The summit still distant
    is reached unerringly
Simply by following
    an alternative way

It is a fine walk
    on a fine day

Elizabeth Clay

Born at Mansfield, Nottinghamshire in 1951, she trained at Nottingham College of Art & Design, Sheffield Polytechnic, Newcastle University and the Royal College of Art. Exhibitions include the *Johnson Matthey Metals Silver Awards* in 1973 & 1976 and again in 1977 when she was a national winner. *Silver Jubilee exhibition*, Abbot Hall, Kendal 1977; *Nature in Art*, Royal College of Art 1977; *Look*, Eli Gern Gallery, Jaffa, Israel 1978; *Craftsmanlike*, Sunderland Arts Centre and National tour 1978; Carlisle Museum & Art Gallery 1980 (a one person touring show); and *Room for Craft*, a Guild of Lakeland Craftsmen touring exhibition 1982.

Poppy and violet bowls, chased silver

Waterfall bowl, silver

Jenny Cowern

Born in 1943, and studied at Brighton and the Royal College of Art. She lectured at Sheffield and Carlisle College of Art.
She was the recipient of Northern Arts production awards in 1974, '76 & '78, and received a major award in 1981. Recent exhibitions include Abbot Hall, Kendal; LYC Museum, Banks, Cumbria and Carlisle Museum & Art Gallery 1980; DLI Museum, Durham; Prescote Gallery, Oxfordshire and Buddle Arts Centre, Wallsend 1981. Publications include *Gallery*, Summer 1980 and *Crafts* Magazine No. 57, July/August 1981.

Sky Felt

Sky Felt 2

Sky study, pastel

John A. Davies

John A. Davies's work is concerned with the exploration of
the natural air/water/landscape.
Since graduating from Trent Polytechnic in 1974 he has managed to
pursue and develop his photography; initially with the help of a number
of minor awards from the Arts Council of Great Britain, to travel around
Ireland, then through various part-time teaching positions.
Since his show at the Photographers' Gallery, London in 1976 he has
shown his work in most of the major photographic galleries in England,
Wales and Ireland. His work has been illustrated in numerous
publications, including a feature in the 1982 *BJP. Annual.*
He has been an active member of North West Arts' Visual Arts Panel in
trying to expand photography in the region.
In 1981 he completed a photographic fellowship at Sheffield (City)
Polytechnic with a major exhibition of his rural and
urban landscape photographs.

Grasmoor towards Crummock Water

Grasmoor towards Isle of Man

Red Tarn towards Ullswater

Helvellyn

Scafell Pike towards Great Gable

Scafell Pike towards Angle Tarn

Mike Davis

Born in 1946, in London. He studied art at St. Martin's School of Art and Hornsey College of Art, obtaining a degree in Fine Art in 1970. In that year he was awarded a fellowship in stained glass by Digswell Arts Trust, and ran a studio at Digswell House in Welwyn Garden City, until 1981, when he moved to Durham. He has exhibited at the Victoria and Albert Museum, the British Craft Centre, the Design Centre, the R.I.B.A. Gallery and the Royal Scottish Museum, who purchased one of his works in 1981. He is an associate of the British Society of Master Glass Painters.

Arc au Ciel

Ian Hamilton Finlay

With drawings by Ian Gardner

Born in 1925 – in the Orkney Islands (some say), or in Nassau, Bahamas. Though his life does not conform to the seeming facts, he has published plays, short stories, poems, cards, booklets, and prints. He lives at Stonypath, Little Sparta, Dunsyre, Lanarkshire, where he and Sue Finlay have made a garden which is now internationally famous. Stone inscriptions, sundials, or other Finlay-collaborations may be found in the garden of the Max Planck Institute, Stuttgart, outside the British Embassy Residence, Bonn, at the Universities of Liège and Canterbury, and in the Botanic Gardens, Edinburgh. The Finlay's own garden (and garden temple) may be visited by prior appointment. His works are normally subject to 'instant arrestment' by Strathclyde Region.
He has no Arts Council grant.

DRIP-DRY
May

MOORLAND
marquetry

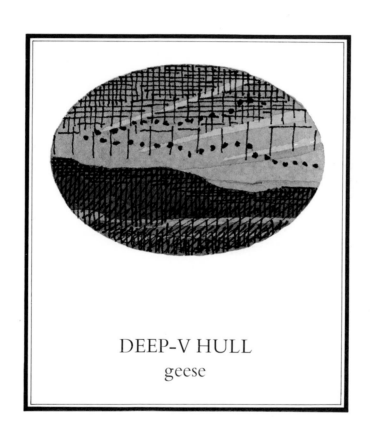

DEEP-V HULL
geese

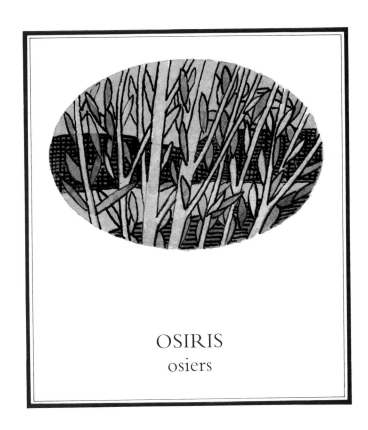

OSIRIS

osiers

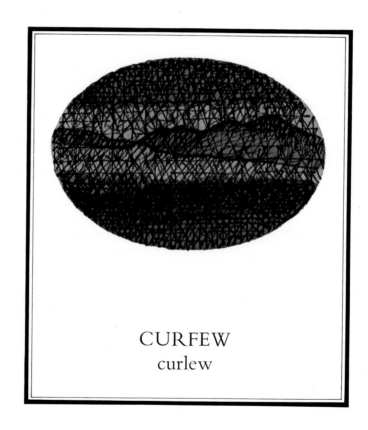

CURFEW
curlew

Hamish Fulton

Born in London in 1946, and grew up in Newcastle upon Tyne. After studying at Hammersmith College of Art, St. Martin's School of Art and the Royal College of Art he travelled in North and South America, Mexico, Iceland, Nepal, India and Australia.
He has had numerous one man exhibitions in Britain, Europe and the USA.
Publications by Hamish Fulton include *Hollow Lane*, Situation Publications, London 1971; *The Sweet Grass Hills of Montana*, Sperone Editore, Turin 1971; Bulletin 52, *Art and Project*, Amsterdam 1972; *Ten Views of Brockmans Mount*, Stedelijk Museum, Amsterdam 1973; *Hamish Fulton*, Galleria Toselli, Milan 1974; *Skyline Ridge*, P. M. J. Self, London 1977; *Nepal 1975*, Van Abbemuseum, Eindhoven 1977; *Nine Works, 1969–1973*, Robert Self, London 1977; and *Roads and Paths*, Schirmer Mosel, Munich 1978.

GREEN ROAD

A SEVEN DAY WALKING JOURNEY FROM PENRITH TO HUDDERSFIELD AUTUMN 1979

HIGH STREET   HELVELLYN   DENT   GREAT WOLD   MASTILES LANE   WITHINS   HEBDEN WATER   BLACKSTONE EDGE

Roy Fisher

Poet and musician, is the author of six books and numerous other works,
including collaborations with the artists Tom Phillips, Derrick Greaves,
Ian Tyson and Ronald King, and translations, recently issued on record,
of the texts of Schubert's major song-cycles. His most recent publications
include *The Thing About Joe Sullivan*, Carcanet New Press (Poetry Book
Society Choice), *Poems 1955–1980*, Oxford University Press and
Consolidated Comedies, Pig Press.

'Neighbours – We'll Not Part Tonight!'

For the Terrible Knitters of Dent

Roll me round on to the stories of the great knittings
That had their place in the foretimes
About the woollen north country
In a smell of straw and peat, and smoky kitchens;

(With a 'clack!' for a sound
We're knitting the houses round).

As the great sheep's eye of the sun slunk down behind the fell
And his thick grey blanket folded its long rows over,
Door after door closed soft as the mighty strode,
Staggered, ran, limped in the dark to their knitting spell.

(With a step for a sound
We're knitting the houses round).

There was Ram's-Back Rachel, black Tick and Tam Tup,
Six-Pin Tidyman, old Twister Gaukroger's grandson,
Little Stitchy Baby and Kitty Curl, Granny Pullock with the straddle legs,
And a long pale idiot man who would knit with his toes: these made the party up;

(With a breath for a sound
We're knitting the houses round).

Then came the girls Pocket and Flitty, and Ribber Wagstaff with his strong thumbs,
Giantess Appleyard in ten petticoats and not perspiring,
And Schoolmaster Weazell with his knitted walking stick,
Come to set all the children their knitting sums.

(With a squeeze for a sound
We're knitting the houses round).

Where was the clicking of laughter then but amid the smoke
When the knitting songs and the knitting stories ran free,
And the mutton-grease fumbled the wool,
And the wool-swaddled babes in the loft began to choke?

(With a laugh for a sound
We're knitting the houses round).

When it's long past midnight, and the yards of knitting enfold
Foot upon stamping foot, not gingerly pressed together,
And the flushed pink faces still mouth out the rows of song
Then the joy of the knitting runs stitches through young and old;

(With a gasp for a sound
We're knitting the houses round).

Then the needles fly faster and faster; wondrous rows fall
Like water from these long-labouring fingers;
Pile on the floor, to the last knitting-hymn, round knees, waists, bosoms, and envelop
All the great passionate ones in a soft, breathing pall

(With a decent veil
We're knitting the houses round).

The Running Changes

Driving northward in February once
on the run, to be clear of the Midlands
in a panic, and ruin of life

I heard the telephones
ring in the air
for the first hundred miles.

But in the afternoon rain I found Sedbergh
and threaded on through it
as a silent close stone lock

that, letting me pass, held back my trouble –
I hoped only it was not gone on ahead
to lie in wait for me by the Tyne. Once through,

the stretch of the road up to Kirkby,
the plainness and dark of it, settled
my stomach; and the sight of Brough

Keep, black as could be, risen in the fields
by the crossroads, made me for that day
my own man, out over cold stripped Stainmore.

Another year,
coming down in peace out of Durham
in a late snowstorm towards sunset,

I met the lorries, headlamps full on,
thrashing their way up over Stainmore
in spray-waves of rosy-tinged slush,

cloud-world behind and below them
filling the valley-botton,
rolling, shot through with pink,

in the side-valleys breaking apart
to lance the pastures right across
with sunlight from no sure source:

and under the last trail of the cloud,
the vanishing up of its blush
into the grey, and the snow thinning,

there, once again,
being dark, was Brough Castle, still
strangely off to one side of the road's change.

Ian Gardner

Born in Lancaster in 1944, and studied at Lancaster and Nottingham Colleges of Art. He has participated in numerous group exhibitions in Britain and abroad. These include *Northern Young Contemporaries*, Whitworth Art Gallery, Manchester 1965, when he was a prizewinner; *Metaphor and Motif*, Midland Group, Nottingham 1972; Serpentine Gallery, London 1973; *Real Life*, Peter Moore's Exhibition, Liverpool 1977; *Works on Paper*, from the Contemporary Art Society's collection, Royal Academy 1977; *The Open and Closed Book*, Victoria and Albert Museum 1979; *The Viewfinders*, Abbot Hall, Kendal 1980; and *Art and the Sea*, ICA, London 1981–82. He has had six one-man shows at the Francis Kyle Gallery, London, and is co-founder of New Arcadians with Patrick Eyres. He has produced work in collaboration with Ian Hamilton Finlay, Jonathan Williams, Thomas A. Clark and Patrick Eyres.

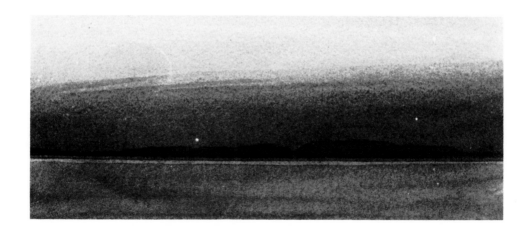

Furness

Borrowdale

Cautley Spout

Honister Pass

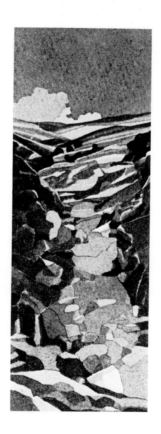

Cowholes

Roger Garfitt

Lives in Sunderland with the poet Frances Horovitz and together they contrive to spend a large part of each winter in a farmhouse near Birdoswald on Hadrian's Wall. He is a poet and critic, and a regular presenter of Radio 3's *Poetry Now*. From 1978 to 1981 he was the Editor of *Poetry Review*. His first collection, *West of Elm*, was published by Carcanet in 1975. His latest poems have recently appeared in a Northern House pamphlet, *The Broken Road*. In 1981 he was one of four poets who collaborated with four artists to produce *Wall*, LYC Press, Banks, Brampton, Cumbria, an exploration on the theme of Hadrian's Wall.

Gardening in Avernus

Evening in the turned earth.
A night wind foxes the grass.
Still through the late afternoon
of stone the thin scent rises
of a herb patch by the wall,
and I am on a path of
that other garden, where thyme
is grey bush beyond the vines,
reptile over the dry rocks.

Cicadas stir the leaf fall.
The lich-owl pronounces dusk
over shadowless cedars.
The foraging pipistrelles
enter meridian blue.
A common scent of earth is
the black ship across Ocean,
a coast of willows and mist.
Without a trench of dark blood

I have come where the tenses
elide. The past re-opens
to a nervous link through an
electronic gate, or the
Gate of Horn. Cell by single
cell an identity wakes,
as over featureless distances
the sightlines form of
particular earth and hours.

Kestrel

When the wind skirmishes
through bracken and winter grass,
a second skirmisher follows,
in camouflage that vanishes
into the red-backed bracken,
the buff feathers of grass;
a bolt from the blue
takes the breath of its kills:

a crossbow
hunts over the low hills;
its shadow goes before it
over bracken and gorse.

Blue

Memory on a peg
behind the door:

the slip-leash a live line
through my fingers

that floats on his shoulders'
running water

or knows their stiffening
the undertow

of another presence
in the hedgebank

still rancorous with fox.
Always that shock

as the hackles rise on
a waking dream,

an ancient line stands out
in the young dog.

Slip him, and I become
the outer ear,

the iris of his eye,
ready to shout

if he conjures a fox
as he stag-leaps

and salmons the long grass.
Enter the land

within the land, a light
and shadow land

whose denizens are quick
and changing shapes,

where the pheasant's wing spreads
into dead wood,

and riddles of brown earth
in the stubble

or clods of bleached-out grass
in the furrow

soon as our backs are turned
go haring off.

Enter the light and dark
of the duel,

the dog's dive and dolphin
over the ground,

a shoulder gleam breaking
the air's surface,

a slate gleam, night closing
with each new stride,

the hare's running rings, her
lucky numbers,

noughts and figures of eight
a breathing space

won on every turn.
Enter the dark

of that other duel
he fought, the leash

an allegiance he held,
a last life line.

Sorrow still rives me that
I let him slip.

Buzzard Soaring

So long grounded

in himself, under such
feather weight

he seems to rise
out of a sack.

A dead poundage
re-assembles on the wings

spread into a sycamore key
turning. Earth breathes him out,

exhales him from his vantage,
to glide with the traffic between worlds,

the exploring galaxies of spores,
the achenes suspended in their shrouds.

The equality, the lightness here . . .
He feels his shadow separate

and travel the air, another
wanderer, another dust.

Below, history fires its
intricate acreage. Demesnes melt.

Towns bleed across ploughland.
Motorways grub like glaciers.

He suns. He sleepwalks on the wing
through this world and the next,

hearing the hormones hiss, hearing
the froth in his cells: *Re-enter*

the inferno. Rise again as ash.

Crows in Snow

Absences of motion, of colour.

Meteorite or moraine, black stones
half-in or half-out of the snow.

Only purpose survives

and has them belly down, black cones
of heat-absorption, solar cells

recharging in the sun

as if all has to be done again,
the ground to disclose its strata,

the minerals their millennia,

the fossil slates of Langenaltheim
split a second time, and flight feathers

print once, twice on the snow.

The Broken Road

Water on the fields
sedged with white grass

Tarmac over flints
the flints wearing through

Walking again
along the broken road:

is it the road bears us up
or the brokenness?

As the upper sky darkens
a depth enters the pools,
corn gold suffuses the grass

The stones grow luminous as they dim

Out of the blue-blacks of the tar
the blues effloresce

Light is a bloom
a pollen of blue

It powders up under our feet

Fay Godwin

Has had no formal training. Her work has been widely exhibited in one-
man shows and is included in many public and private collections both
here and in USA, and elsewhere abroad.
Co-author of *The Oldest Road*, An Exploration of the Ridgeway, with
J. R. L. Anderson in 1975; *The Oil Rush*, with Mervyn Jones 1976;
The Drovers Roads of Wales with Shirley Toulson 1977; *Islands* with
John Fowles 1978; *Remains of Elmet* with Ted Hughes 1979;
Romney Marsh with Richard Ingrams 1980. Currently working on
The Whisky Roads of Scotland with Derek Cooper, and
The Saxon Shore Way with Alan Sillitoe.
Selected collections, Victoria & Albert Museum, London, Bibliotheque
Nationale, Paris, the Department of the Environment, London, National
Portrait Gallery, London, Arts Council of Great Britain, Mappin Gallery,
Sheffield, Royal Library, Copenhagen.

These Cumbrian pictures are for Neil Hanson.

Seathwaite Fell from Green Gable

Gillercomb Head from Green Gable

Winter Tree, Derwentwater

Wastwater Screes

Bollard, Harrington Marina

Castlerigg

Andy Goldsworthy

Born in 1956. He trained at Bradford Art College and Preston Polytechnic. Since leaving College in 1978, he has lived in Morecambe, Bentham, Nr. Lancaster and Ilkley, West Yorkshire, living and working in each place for about a year. In August 1981 he moved to Brough, Cumbria, where he now works. Exhibitions include *Nature as Material* 1980 (Arts Council touring exhibition), L.Y.C. Museum, Banks, Cumbria 1980 (one man), Serpentine Gallery Summer Show 1981.

Icicle and rock, Brough

Grass stalks and damp elm leaves, Brough

Balanced rocks, Morecambe Bay

Broken, reconstructed stone, Morecambe Bay

Five stones, Scafell Pike

Richard Harris

Born at Newton Abbot, Devon in 1954. He studied at Torquay and Gloucestershire College of Art. He was appointed Grizedale Forest Sculptor in Residence in 1977–78. He travelled and worked in Australia from 1979 to 1981, lecturing at various art schools and was resident sculptor at 'Birrigai' School (40 km from Canberra). He exhibited at the First Australian Sculpture Triennial, Melbourne, 1981. Publications include *Aspects* 7, and *Art and Australia*, March 1982.

Cliff structure, Grizedale Forest

Tony Harrison

Poet, born in Leeds 1937. His mother's family Wilkinson lived in Martindale for centuries, mainly at Thrang Crag. Tony Harrison's publications include: POETRY: *The Loiners*, 1970, *Palladas: Poems*, 1975, *from The School of Eloquence* and other poems, 1978, and most recently *Continuous*, Rex Collings 1981, from which *Lines to my Grandfathers* is taken. THEATRE: *The Misanthrope*, 1973, *Phaedra Britannica*, 1975, *Bow Down*, 1977, *The Passion*, 1977, *The Oresteia*, Rex Collings 1981, all of which were produced by the National Theatre.

Lines to my Grandfathers

1

Ploughed parallel as print the stony earth.
The straight stone walls defy the steep grey slopes.
The place's rightness for my mother's birth
exceeds the pilgrim grandson's wildest hopes –

Wilkinson farmed Thrang Crag, Martindale.

Horner was the Haworth signalman.

Harrison kept a pub with home-brewed ale,

Fell-farmer, railwayman and publican,

and he, while granma slaved to tend the vat
graced the rival bars 'to make comparisons',
Queen's Arms, the Duke of this, the Duke of that,
while his was known as just 'The Harrison's'.

He carried cane and *guineas*, no coin baser!
He dressed the gentleman beyond his place
and paid in gold for beer and whisky chaser
but took his knuckleduster, just in case.

2

The one who lived with us was grampa Horner
who, I remember, when a sewer rat
got driven into our dark cellar corner
booted it to pulp and squashed it flat.

He cobbled all our boots. I've got his last.
We use it as a doorstop on warm days.
My present is propped open by their past
and looks out over straight and narrow ways:

the way one ploughed his land, one squashed a rat,
kept railtracks clear, or, dressed up to the nines
with waxed moustache, gold chain, his cane, his hat,
drunk as a lord could foot it on straight lines.

Fell farmer, railwayman and publican,
I strive to keep my lines direct and straight,
and try to make connections where I can –

the knuckleduster's now my paperweight!

John Hilliard

Born, Lancaster, 1945. Trained as a sculptor at St. Martin's School Of Art, London, but has worked with the medium of photography for the last 12 years. Northern Arts Fellow in Visual Art, 1976–78. Regular one-man exhibitions in Europe and North America since 1970, and group exhibitions including *The New Art*, Hayward Gallery, London 1972; Paris Biennale, Musée D'Art Moderne, Paris 1977; *Documenta 6*, Kassel 1977; Vienna Biennale, Vienna Secession 1981. Lives in London and teaches at Brighton Polytechnic.

Langdale Fell

Towards Thirlmere

THE RIGG

The Rigg

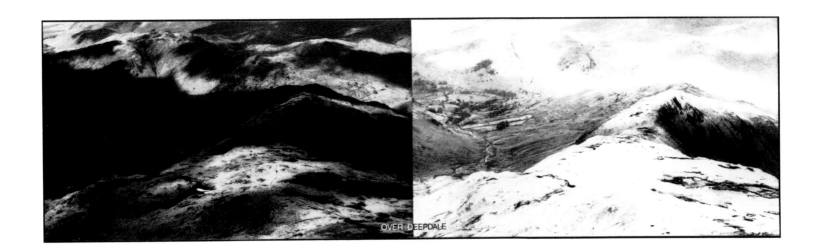

OVER DEEPDALE

Over Deepdale

Julia Hills

Has been making dolls since childhood. She was born in Surrey in 1944.
She studied theatre design at Croydon Art School, then worked as a
buyer for Sadlers Wells Theatre wardrobe, and as a seamstress for a
theatrical costumier. For three years she worked at the Thorndike Theatre
where she designed and made all the costumes.
In 1970 she left the theatre to do a course in community and youth work,
after that she moved to Newcastle upon Tyne where in 1975 she began
making dolls full time. In 1979 she returned south to live in London.
She now lives in a Craft Community in the Cotswolds. She is on the
Craft Council's Index of Craftsmen and has exhibited her work
throughout the country. She also runs dollmaking weekend workshops.
Member of British Craft Centre, Guild of Lakeland Craftsmen,
and Toymakers Guild.

Spring and Winter, (details)

Frances Horovitz

Widely known as a broadcaster and as a presenter of poetry in live performance. The most recent collection of her own poetry is *Water Over Stone* from the Enitharmon Press, Autumn 1980. She is also one of the four poets who contributed to *Wall*, LYC Press. Publications in 1982 include *Rowlstone Haiku*, written jointly with Roger Garfitt and published by the Five Seasons Press, Hereford; a selection of poems in *Bread and Roses*, an anthology of women's poetry from Virago; and poems in Secker and Warburg's forthcoming Cornish anthology, edited by Peter Redgrove.

Finding a Sheep's Skull

Sudden glimpse of bone
at the path's edge
like a larger mushroom,
almost hidden by leaves.

I handle the skull gently
shaking out earth and spiders.
Loose teeth chock in the jaw:
it smells of nothing.

I hold it up to sunlight,
a grey-green translucent shell.
Light pours in
        like water
through blades and wafers of bone.
        In secret caves
filaments of skull hang down;
frost and rain have worked
        to shredded lace.

The seasons waste its symmetry.
        It is a cathedral
echoing spring; in its decay
        plainsong of lamb
        and field and sun
inhabits bone.

The shallow cranium
fits in my palm

– for speculative children
I bring it home.

January

A sealed stillness
– only the stream moves,
tremor and furl of water
under dead leaves.

In silence
the wood declares itself;
angles and arabesques of darkness,
branch, bramble,
tussocks of ghost grass
– under my heel
ice shivers
frail blue as sky
between the runes of trees.

Far up
rooks, crows
flail home.

Sightings

Flake on flake, snow
packed light as ash
        or feather,
shavings of crystal.
    By moonlight
stars pulse underfoot.

    The burning fox ran here,
his narrow print
      under gate
         and over wall
diagonal across the field;
    skeining of rabbit tracks,
our own slurred trail.

    Like black stones
crows squat, sunning
      among staring sheep
– crow's wing
      brushed on snow,
three strokes
      twice etched
as faint and fine
      as fossil bone.

A Dream

for Winifred Nicholson

Flowers,
a dozen or more,
I picked one summer afternoon
from field and hedgerow.
Resting against a wall
I held them up
to hide the sun.
Cell by cell,
exact as dance,
I saw the colour,
structure, purpose
of each flower.
I named them with their secret names.
They flamed in air.

    But, waking
I remember only two
– soapwort and figwort,
the lilac and the brown.
The rest I guess at
but cannot see
– only myself,
almost a ghost upon the road,
without accoutrement,
holding the flowers
as torch and talisman
against the coming dark.

for Stephen Procter

on seeing his exhibition of forms in glass

Perfected whiteness
– a stellar littoral, bright
beyond bone or pearl.

Spiral chambers sing of
sea's breath, the curve
and fall of flowers.

Cave within a cave
of quiet, thought becomes music;
litanies of light resolve

in gathering trance.
A whorl of shadow
trembles, brims.

Oh wave and silence,
breaking still
in shining arcs of air.

The Crooked Glen

I saw nothing but waves and winds

. . . the moon resting in a broken apple tree
an ushering wind shake ash and alder
by the puckered river.
Lightly, like boats, the thin leaves rock and spin.

Blood-dark berries stir; above my head the thorn trees lean.
In their black pools the moon fragments herself.

Ghost dry the unquiet reeds . . .

I saw nothing but the waters wap

and waves wan

Camboglanna or the Crooked Glen at Birdoswald is one of
the reputed sites of Arthur's last battle.

Paul Joyce

Born at Winchester, Hampshire in 1940 and was educated at Dulwich
College. In addition to his photography, he has directed documentaries
for Universal, Paramount and Twentieth Century Fox, and has directed
plays and films from scripts by Samuel Beckett, Tom Stoppard, Joe
Orton and Harold Pinter. He has co-authored with Peter Terson the play
Love us and Leave us, and wrote and directed the BBC Play for Today
Keep Smiling. He has exhibited at the Photography Gallery, Southampton
in 1977 and *Elders* at the National Portrait Gallery in 1978, when the
British Council toured a show of his landscapes in Europe. The major
retrospective *From Age to Age* was mounted by the Welsh Arts Council in
1980 and his work was included in British Art 1940–80, at the Hayward
Gallery in 1981. He has also shown at the Bibliotheque Nationale, Paris in
1980 and Contrasts Gallery, London 1982. The Victoria & Albert
acquired a portfolio of his work in 1976.

The Vale of the Black Horse

Downwards from Fell End to Rawthey

Stennerskeugh Clouds

Limestone Skull, (Cloud upon Cloud)

Walk 22, (for A.W.)

Brant Fell – Arant Haw – Winder

The Black Hole of Busha, (for J.W.)

David Nathan Kemp

Painter, sculptor, assembler and dissembler has worked as a merchant
seaman, junior executive, tree surgeon, ships chandler, sea-side
photographer and antique restorer. He attended Farnham Art School and
Wimbledon School of Art 1967–72. He has lived by the sea
in West Cornwall since 1978.
He has works in the Nuffield Foundation and the Arts Council permanent
collection. Recent exhibitions include *The 1980 Squeaky Floor Show*,
Newlyn Orion, Penzance; *Public Hanging*, Penwith Gallery, St. Ives; and
the Arts Council touring exhibition *Fragments against Ruins*. He was
resident sculptor at Grizedale Forest, April–September 1981.

Rook Crossing, Grizedale Forest, (detail)

Scale Green Birdman, Grizedale Forest

Carryin' Crow

Geoffrey Key

In collaboration with Susanna Birley

Born in Manchester in 1941. After studying at the Regional College of
Art, Manchester where he was awarded the Heywood Medal in Fine Art,
Guthrie Bond Scholarship, he took a post-diploma in sculpture. In 1978
an illustrated monograph on Geoffrey Key's work was published.
Selected one-man exhibitions include Salford Art Gallery 1966, '69, '72 &
'76; Sheffield University 1979; Erica Bourne Gallery, London 1974;
Vision 35 Gallery, Nancy, France 1974; Gallery 39 Manchester 1978;
Lausanne Switzerland 1980. Group exhibitions have included the
Manchester Annual Exhibition since 1971 (when he won the first prize),
Salon d'Automne, Clermont-Ferrand, France (A three-man show with
L. S. Lowry & Harold Riley), Galerie Tendenz, Germany 1977, Royal
Northern College of Music 1978, Art Expo, New York 1980.

Beehive form, Albarello and Dish

Thomas Meyer

Born in Seattle in 1947. Since graduating from Bard College in 1969, he
has divided his time between North Carolina and Northern England.
His books include: *The Bang Book*, Jargon Society 1972, *The Umbrella of
Aesculapius*, Jargon Society 1975, *Uranian Roses*, Catalyst 1977 and *Staves,
Calends, Legends*, Jargon Society 1979.

Calends

At dusk iridescent
starlings swarm with slugs,
spiders, snails in their beaks.

Stones house noise
in the eaves' gaps, hollows
of moss lined straw, dry grass,

demanding young, ugly,
fat & hungry.

Sheep bleat, dog bark.
Far call of peewit, rook.

Bouquets of lilac & ajuga,
    mouse-ear & sprays
of white hawthorn mays
    arranged in kilner jars

Empty corners flooded
    by columns, spiralling
motes, flecks of shadows
    from green elder

Sweet smells on moist air,
    clouds over Helms Knott,
rain on window ledge

The new hewn lintel admits
sunlight

summer's hedges are laid, lithe
saplings bent back, threaded in

tender, unfurled bracken fronds

shelter an indwelling, verdant
articulation

nets of enclosure, stinted
allotments

dry, blue-rag walls

A grotto of rocks thick with moss where
leaves bower hidden aethers, ladened air
that opens up deep chambers
lighting the mind's cave

They are the doorflag & architrave,
inroad under a stead,
passage to something
tremulous, vibrating, fleet

A faint glist lifts the haze.
Incandescence wraps each pore.
Webs cast up, seeds lost in
the word hoard

            replicas
of distant, clouded soundings
housed by shining husks

            foliate
blazons

        Plait the cord
        knot & cross
        tie it off
        with acorn bobbin

Bee & spider
rowan, pimpernel
sinegreen
cold iron

        Rushlight
        shrinks the room
        extends
        the outer margin

Vocatus adque non vocatus deus aderit

Pausing, head turned, the beast sees
what beckons
        horsetail & horns
bison head, cloven hoof,

       flute music

men in chamois disguise leap

       By torchlight & smoke
red ochre handprint,
       chipped flint, bear
skull & bones in coffers, apron,
bracelet, crown of nassas, disks,
ivory rings, trochus shells

       lush evidence

of a dance

footfall & beat, ancient sun
striking stone

       Grass on the flanks,
up Winder, the Calf, down Cautley
by Rawthey Bridge

ghost of a broken stone circle

Song of skylark high off Bram Rigg Top
scores the air,
fades like slender
rushes brought down fells
dry, strewn over flags to
sweeten the house.

June gloam settles on Holme Fell,
a casual heap
of earth & rock, ramparts
where huts ringed
a green hollow. The half-light
turns to shadow.

Gypsies' caravans pulled up
in a clearing
off the lane by the Lune
near Otter Wood,
dusk thickens & vanishes
in their camp fire.

Cross-shaft carved
with a figure bound
in interlace, Loki
netted

disjointed webbing,
twists of threads
& cast up images

Stone beaks peck stone fruit,
Bewcastle's cross
designs the rime

vine scrolls & knotwork

patterns interweaving
the lines, dense,
intricate scheme

rendering it whole,

lift & fall like a heron's wing

Scattered wall stones,
clumps of cowparsley,
nettles & cat mint

flies swarm,
rise in black clouds
above fresh cow dung

Day reaches ripeness in sunlight

doors open & admit
a bright dust
to its original source

the air swells,
gathering sparks,
the house fills
with a seed fire lost
by hesitant glance

Dark corners center,
each shape quakes

empty spaces shine,
invoked, embodied

Ian McKeever

Born at Withernsea, East Yorkshire in 1946. He studied at Avery College
of Education, London. His one man exhibitions include ICA, London
1973; Ikon Gallery, Birmingham; and Galleria del Cavallino, Venice
1976 and 1980; Nigel Greenwood Gallery, 1977, '79, '81; Spectro Arts,
Newcastle; Richard Demarco, Edinburgh; Galleria Tommaseo, Trieste;
Galleria Akumulatory, Poznan; Galleria Foksal, Warsaw 1979; Arnolfini,
Bristol; Third Eye Centre, Glasgow; ICA, London;
Walker Art Gallery, Liverpool 1980.
He was Artist in residence at the Bridewell Studio, Liverpool 1980–81,
and in Nuremberg, West Germany 1981–82.

Night Flak – Mark Glad Departure Day

Raymond Moore

Born in Wallasey, Cheshire in 1920. He was initially trained as a painter at the Royal College of Art and started teaching photography in 1956. In 1970 he travelled to America and met Minor White, Harry Callahan and Aaron Siskind. Began teaching photography at Trent Polytechnic, Nottingham in 1975. In 1977 he was awarded a major Bursary by the Arts Council of Great Britain. He resigned from his position at Trent Polytechnic in 1978 and moved to Carlisle, Cumbria to concentrate on his own work. He has exhibited widely in Britain and the USA. Major publications include: *Raymond Moore*, Welsh Arts Council catalogue 1968; *Camera*, C. J. Bucher, Lucerne, Switzerland 1977; *Murmurs at Every Turn, The Photographs of Raymond Moore*, Travelling Light, London 1981. Public collections include Art Institute of Chicago, USA, Bibliotheque Nationale, Paris, Gurnsheim Collection, Austin, Texas, Victoria & Albert Museum, London, Arts Council of Great Britain.

Maryport

Allonby

Maryport

Allonby

Allonby

Silloth

Frank Nelson

Born in Blackpool in 1930 and studied at Blackpool Art School. He has worked as a fitter in the aircraft industry, on design and mouldmaking for TVR, and has produced models of sailing ships, replica armour, industrial models for the British Aircraft Corporation, props for films such as *Star Wars*, *Barry Lyndon* and *A Bridge Too Far*, and worked for three years at Blackpool Pleasure Beach in charge of modelmaking and animations. He now devotes himself full time to his own work living at Hebden Bridge, Yorkshire. Exhibitions include *Summer Show*, Serpentine Gallery, London 1979, *Wood*, Ceolfrith Gallery, Sunderland Arts Centre and national tour 1981, and Grundy House Gallery, Blackpool 1982. He contributed to an international wood carving seminar at Parnham House in 1982.

Langdale Axe Factory

Brendan Neiland

Born at Lichfield, Staffordshire in 1941. He studied at Birmingham
College of Art and the Royal College of Art where he was awarded the
John Minton Scholarship. He has had numerous one man and group
exhibitions in Britain and the USA. Selected Public Collections are Arts
Council of Great Britain, British Council, Victoria & Albert Museum,
Gulbenkian Foundation, Contemporary Arts Society, Print Collection
Tate Gallery, Toronto Art Gallery, Boston Museum of Fine Art,
Brooklyn Museum, New York.

Cumbrian landscape 1

Cumbrian landscape 2

David Nash

Born in England in 1945, he lives and works in Blaenau Ffestiniog,
North Wales.
He has had numerous one man and group exhibitions in Britain, Europe
and the USA. Collections include Kroller Muller Museum, Holland,
Guggenheim Museum, New York, and public and private collections
in Britain and Europe.
Peter Francis Brown has produced the film *Woodman*, about
David Nash, whose publications include *Loosely held Grain*, 1976
and *Fletched over Ash*, 1978.

Stone stove, Cumbria, 'a meeting of ways', Grizedale Forest

Stone stove, Cumbria, Grizedale Forest

Wooden waterway, Grizedale Forest

Running table, Grizedale Forest

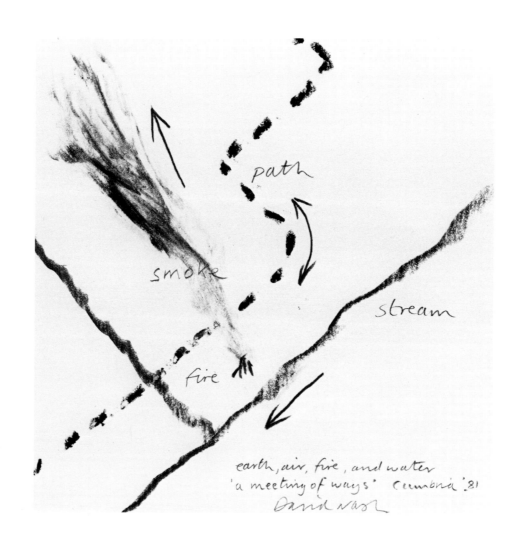

path

smoke

stream

fire

earth, air, fire, and water
'a meeting of ways' Cumbria '81
David Nash

Earth, air, fire, and water, 'a meeting of ways'

Norman Nicholson

Was born in 1914 at Millom, Cumberland, in the house where he still lives. His first book of poems, *Five Rivers*, gained the Heinemann Prize for 1945, while his most recent collection, *Sea to the West*, Fabers, was the Poetry Book Society's Summer Choice for 1981. As well as eight books of verse, he has published a critical biography of the poet William Cowper, and written or edited a number of books on the topography and literary history of Cumbria, including *Portrait of the Lakes*, Hale, *The Lakers*, Hale and *The Lake District: An Anthology*, Penguin. Norman Nicholson received a Cholmondeley Award in 1967 and the Queen's Medal for Poetry in 1977, together with honorary degrees of M.A. from Manchester and the Open Universities and an honorary Doctorate from Liverpool University 1980.
He was awarded an O.B.E. in the Birthday Honours 1981.

To the River Duddon

I wonder, Duddon, if you still remember
An oldish man with a nose like a pony's nose,
Broad bones, legs long and lean but strong enough
To carry him over Hard Knott at seventy years of age.
He came to you first as a boy with a fishing-rod
And a hunk of Ann Tyson's bread and cheese in his pocket,
Walking from Hawkshead across Walna Scar;
Then as a middle-aged Rydal landlord,
With a doting sister and a government sinecure,
Who left his verses gummed to your rocks like lichen,
The dry and yellow edges of a once-green spring.
He made a guide-book for you, from your source
There where you bubble through the moss on Wrynose
(Among the ribs of bald and bony fells
With screes scratched in the turf like grey scabs),
And twist and slither under humpbacked bridges –
Built like a child's house from odds and ends
Of stones that lie about the mountain side –
Past Cockley Beck Farm and on to Birk's Bridge,
Where the rocks stride about like legs in armour,
And the steel birches buckle and bounce in the wind
With a crinkle of silver foil in the crisp of the leaves;
On then to Seathwaite, where like a steam-navvy
You shovel and slash your way through the gorge
By Wallabarrow Crag, broader now
From becks that flow out of black upland tarns
Or ooze through golden saxifrage and the roots of rowans;
Next Ulpha, where a stone dropped from the bridge
Swims like a tadpole down thirty feet of water
Between steep skirting-boards of rock; and thence
You dribble into lower Dunnerdale
Through wet woods and wood-soil and woodland flowers,
Tutson, the St. John's-wort with a single yellow bead,
Marsh marigold, creeping jenny and daffodils;
Here from hazel islands in the late spring
The catkins fall and ride along the stream
Like little yellow weasels, and the soil is loosed
From bulbs of the white lily that smells of garlic,
And dippers rock up and down on rubber legs,
And long-tailed tits are flung through the air like darts;
By Foxfield now you taste the salt in your mouth,

And thrift mingles with the turf, and the heron stands
Watching the wagtails. Wordsworth wrote:
'Remote from every taint of sordid industry'.
But you and I know better, Duddon.
For I, who've lived for nearly thirty years
Upon your shore, have seen the slagbanks slant
Like screes into the sand, and watched the tide
Purple with ore back up the muddy gullies,
And wiped the sinter dust from the farmyard damsons.
A hundred years of floods and rain and wind
Have washed your rocks clear of his words again,
Many of them half-forgotten, brimming the Irish Sea,
But that which Wordsworth knew, even the old man
When poetry had failed like desire, was something
I have yet to learn, and you, Duddon,
Have learned and re-learned to forget and forget again.
Not the radical, the poet and heretic,
To whom the water-forces shouted and the fells
Were like a blackboard for the scrawls of God,
But the old man, inarticulate and humble,
Knew that eternity flows in a mountain beck –
The long cord of the water, the shepherd's numerals
That run upstream, through the singing decades of dialect.
He knew, beneath mutation of year and season,
Flood and drought, frost and fire and thunder,
The blossom on the rowan and the reddening of the berries,
There stands the base and root of the living rock,
Thirty thousand feet of solid Cumberland.

The Black Guillemot

Midway between Fleswick and St Bees North Head,
The sun in the west,
All Galloway adrift on the horizon;
The sandstone red
As dogwood; sea-pink, sea campion and the sea itself
Flowering in clefts of the cliff –
And down on one shelf,
Dozen on dozen pressed side by side together,
White breast by breast,
Beaks to the rock and tails to the fish-stocked sea,
The guillemots rest

Restlessly. Now and then,
One shifts, clicks free of the cliff,
Wings whirling like an electric fan –
Silhouette dark from above, with under-belly gleaming
White as it banks at the turn –
Dives, scoops, skims the water,
Then, with all Cumberland to go at, homes
To the packed slum again,
The rock iced with droppings.

I swing my binoculars into the veer of the wind,
Sight, now, fifty yards from shore,
That rarer auk: all black,
But for two white patches where the wings join the back,
Alone like an off-course migrant
(Not a bird of his kind
Nesting to the south of him in England),

Yet self-subsistent as an Eskimo,
Taking the huff if so much as a feather
Lets on his pool and blow-hole
In the floating pack-ice of gulls.

But, turn the page of the weather,
Let the moon haul up the tides and the pressure-hose of spray
Swill down the lighthouse lantern – then,
When boats keep warm in harbour and bird-watchers in bed,
When the tumble-home of the North Head's rusty hull
Takes the full heave of the storm,
The hundred white and the one black flock
Back to the same rock.

Wall

The wall walks the fell –
Grey millipede on slow
Stone hooves;
Its slack back hollowed
At gulleys and grooves,
Or shouldering over
Old boulders
Too big to be rolled away.
Fallen fragments
Of the high crags
Crawl in the walk of the wall.

A dry-stone wall
Is a wall and a wall,
Leaning together
(Cumberland-and-Westmorland
Champion wrestlers),
Greening and weathering,
Flank by flank,
With filling of rubble
Between the two –
A double-rank
Stone dyke:
Flags and through-
stones jutting out sideways,
Like the steps of a stile.

A wall walks slowly.
At each give of the ground,
Each creak of the rock's ribs,
It puts its foot gingerly,
Arches its hog-holes,
Lets cobble and knee-joint
Settle and grip.
As the slipping fellside
Erodes and drifts,
The wall shifts with it,
Is always on the move.

They built a wall slowly,
A day a week;
Built it to stand,
But not stand still.
They built a wall to walk.

Cloud on Black Combe

The air clarifies. Rain
Has clocked off for the day.

The wind scolds in from Sligo,
Ripping the calico-grey from a pale sky.
Black Combe holds tight
To its tuft of cloud, but over the three-legged island
All the west is shining.

An hour goes by,
And now the starched collars of the eastern pikes
Streak up into a rinse of blue. Every
Inland fell is glinting;
Black Combe alone still hides
Its bald, bleak forehead, balaclava'd out of sight.

Slick fingers of wind
Tease and fidget at wool-end and wisp,
Picking the mist to bits.
Strings and whiskers
Fray off from the cleft hill's
Bilberried brow, disintegrate, dissolve
Into blue liquidity –
Only a matter of time
Before the white is wholly worried away
And Black Combe starts to earn its name again.

But where, in the west, a tide
Of moist and clear-as-a-vacuum air is piling
High on the corried slopes, a light
Fret and haar of hazy whiteness
Sweats off the cold rock; in a cloudless sky
A cloud emulsifies,
Junkets on sill and dyke.
Wool-end and wisp materialize
Like ectoplasm, are twined
And crocheted to an off-white,
Over-the-lughole hug-me-tight;
And Black Combe's ram's-head, butting at the bright
Turfed and brackeny brine,
Gathers its own wool, plucks shadow out of shine.

What the wind blows away
The wind blows back again.

Scafell Pike

Look
Along the well
Of the street,
Between the gasworks and the neat
Sparrow-stepped gable
Of the Catholic chapel,
High
Above tilt and crook
Of the tumbledown
Roofs of the town –
Scafell Pike,
The tallest hill in England.

How small it seems,
So far away,
No more than a notch
On the plate-glass window of the sky!
Watch
A puff of kitchen smoke
Block out peak and pinnacle –
Rock-pie of volcanic lava
Half a mile thick
Scotched out
At the click of an eye.

Look again
In five hundred, a thousand or ten
Thousand years:
A ruin where
The chapel was; brown
Rubble and scrub and cinders where
The gasworks used to be;
No roofs, no town,
Maybe no men;
But yonder where a lather-rinse of cloud pours down
The spiked wall of the sky-line, see,
Scafell Pike
Still there.

Roger Palmer

Born in Portsmouth in 1946. He studied at Portsmouth and Chelsea Schools of Art. After teaching in the Department of Fine Art at Newcastle University, he became Artist/Photographer in Residence at Trent Polytechnic, Nottingham in 1977–78. He currently lives in Nottinghamshire. His one-man exhibitions include Angela Flowers, London 1976 & '77; Oliver Dowling, Dublin 1976 & '78; Sunderland Arts Centre 1979; Moira Kelly Gallery, London 1981. Group exhibitions include *Time, Words and the Camera*, Kunstlerhaus, Graz 1976–77; *Aspects of the Landscape*, A British Council touring exhibition 1977–79; *Art Landscape/Landscape Art*, Hodvikodden, Oslo, 1978; *Three Perspectives on Photography*, Hayward Gallery, London 1979 and ROSC '80, University College, Dublin 1980.

SKIDDAW

A 3054 FT. MOUNTAIN

BELOW PILLAR MOUNTAIN

A VALLEY OF DARK CONIFERS

A SOURCE OF THREE INDUSTRIAL RIVERS

A NATURAL BORDER BETWEEN ENGLAND AND SCOTLAND

MARYPORT   WORKINGTON   WHITEHAVEN

INDUSTRIAL TOWNS ON THE SOLWAY FIRTH

MUCKLE SAMUEL'S CRAGS

ON THE EDGE OF BRITAIN'S LARGEST MAN-MADE FOREST

Rodney Pybus

Born in Newcastle upon Tyne in 1938. He read English and Classics at
Cambridge and has worked as a journalist, television writer and producer
and university lecturer. He was Literature Officer for Cumbria 1979–81
and Writer in Residence, North Tyneside 1982.
Collections of poetry include: *In Memoriam Milena*, Chatto & Windus
1973, (Awarded Alice Hart Bartlett Prize by the Poetry Society); *Bridging
Loans*, Chatto & Windus 1976 and *The Loveless Letters* (Chatto & Windus
1981). He was represented in *Wall* (Ed. Noel Connor, LYC Press 1981)
and co-edited with William Scammell *Adam's Dream*
(Cumbria Literature 1981).

A Durable Music

Most walls now are prose
defining private places –
our insubstantial theories
of domesticity, work
or loneliness held in place
by the rational argument of bricks,
chunky with imperatives.
Mortar may overcivilise
the sensible heart.
Most walls now are prose.

But some are an old poet's work,
undulant and epic forms
tongued and hearted to perfection
in slate or stone's own rhythm,
not a cadence out of shape.
Some master of the long dry line
has measured his craft against the fells,
a true hyperborean makar.
I see his grey muse striding
through the north's bold weather,
inspired curlews rhyming
with the wind.

Elterwater

for Arthur Evans

I watch water, peat, and willows
drowning in the wait for December,
the lake of the wild swans hushed.
A long breath before music.

Out of their island of ice and fire
come the swans, chuting from the tundra
of the upper air like feathered shells;
plane the calm glide of Elptarvatn

to rest. Canopies fold over
rippled glass and each bent whoop
of a neck that bugled in flight
dips for plants, whose shining

flowers will whiten the spring,
late snowflakes underwater,
not dissolving but blooming.
In such a place the old sailors

turned finally to the hills;
those horned men, blazing from sunset,
made harbour of bouldered water,
dismal screes, a thwaite for storm-

bitten shepherds, naming this
guttural unlatinate North
where I have come back,
feeling the ache of cold roots;

feel least an alien. O
let me never hear the true swan-song
they say's like the heart of a dying fall:
from the failing trachea gravity
and death haul out an octave.

The Year of the White Horse

My dear, this last, the Chinese might say,
has been the Year of the White Horse:
one we saw together in that world's-end
southern Arcadia, put out to grass,
the misplaced winter sun of June
tipping its mellowing slow light
the colour of paw-paw juice
over his flanks, his wise heftiness
and gaze so watchful he might have grown
unbroken in that sage green paddock.
From another hemisphere I see him blaze.

And a mare last month turning to grey
with the year, her foal radiating
through the mist, brisk as frost,
wheeling and bucking the weight
of the sky; ourselves between seasons.

Forty years tonight: half of them
circling round us, these white
marital threads, consonant wedded hours.
So long touching, we've sometimes flashed
like stripped wires,
sometimes felt our growing
together as natural as grass itself.

This year's been out of kilter,
winter kicking straight into winter
as we came home, tugged
by the old magnet of North
and its long incurable vocation.
At rest for the moment on the deciduous green
edge of this mild peninsula of Ultima Thule,
your lovely breath mists in cool intimations;
white horses begin to catch
the scent of spring's quick rooting.

From the fell-side we watch the tide's
own white horses gathering
for the next drive across the sands.
And I remember from before I met you
the confusion of the Latin sea in print:
mare and mare! – this improbable, still
curiously exciting overlapping of tongues.

Not Only Forms

Not long since, we combed
the shoreline of this western foreland
among the jetsam of weather, tide
and all things that diminish
through the hourglass of air,

trying for purchase
on the sliding stones, these difficult
peninsular relics,
rounded bones
and pounded forms
of the earth's violent slow decay –

a place where crows come in their black
twilight clusters
for raucous scouring
and picking over;

hammer in hand, mind pacing,
you fossicked for spoors
of what's locked, original,

oldest lithographs
of what brought us here
to the mad pebble-dashed hurtle
of this planet.

Always the continuing
preamble of form:

the curt consonance
of stones, their milled gravel
under-foot, and the tide's drawn
vowel receding
over the bay's wide tongue,

those sombre mud-flats
that take the earth right out
to meet the sky:
a complex speech
you tried for size, attesting

to weighed syllables
and potential music.

One lumpen limestone block
the sea'd rolled smooth
you split with a blow,
surprised the quick faint scent
of ancient chemistry escaping,
and found each half sharing
the fossil's image,
bi-valve across the break –
delicate drypoint
of a radiating fan
in its storm of stone:
both image and narrative.

Presiding friend, hierophant
of authentic making,
you held to the joy
of insight striking, not
only the entrancing rigid forms;

later, you gave me half,
a gift to match across
the break. In return
I bring you this, less durable
but form of a kind, this still hardening speech.

Yes, a gift against the times.

Heron (1)

I go out in all grey weather
to the bay of a wide afternoon,
where the skin is drawn slowly
back from a crescent mile of mud;
see him standing there, image of his water-
coloured self, knee-deep
in the swirl and drag of water
sliding out of reach.

Like a sand-pilot with no followers
he leans over his stilts, hunching
for the long wait of afternoon;
leans on himself and
striking for fish
misses: the moment passes but
the ripples seem never quite to fade
from the ebbing tide, like water
poured on paper the brush has marked.

Soon he'll hoist into the dusk
till I'm a dark pebble on the far shore;
his great wings painting himself into sky,
he'll go calling 'kark, kark!' like the coarse
throat of night crying for still more dark.

Heron (2)

First, I see him turning
with the tide, coasting over
marsh and alluvial meadows
green with the under-water hopeful
light of showers swathed across the fells;
then settled, dark as slate against
the brighter sea, watch-keeper
of his own lean tower, hawkish-eyed
for slow fish, whatever unsubtle moves.
Thin-shanked as reeds but firmly
isolate, brooding over the sliding
of water past him.

Gulls pass in a storm of white
and busy shouting, their hunger
brusque and patent in the falling light.
Feathering the currents, he lifts,
calling twice, this time deceived.
Watching him go and turn
his plumage into night, I think
I aim myself for such
considered, cunning flight.

Almanac of Herons

Time suspends its long neck
over the recoiling tide.
Minutes will uncover these grains of world
where I at the boundary hazard my self.

They know what this queer stillness
is all about, the three herons:
this reprise of the future,
the inquisitive pace of its advent.

On thin-shanked wits
Death leans with present grace.
They know the weight of a second

when things are to be quickened.
Feathering the wasted sunlight,
the grey sky opens its wings
and flaps upwards, greedy for night and silence.

The birds ponder over the frothy seepage
and minute particulars of water,

yawn like judges, and
preen their talents and poise.
Seconds flutter and settle
their slimy sheen
over the bald spinning of this pebble-world.

One flies overhead
shouting *kark! kark!*
circling the dark growing all the time
darker, presents
a swathe of dark pinions,
its minatory spear to the west.

The imperfect future drains
without echo from the shore.

Edward Ranney

Born in 1942 and educated at Yale and Columbia Universities.
His fellowships include Fulbright Fellowship to Cuzco, Peru 1964–65;
National Endowment for the Arts 1975; John Simon Guggenheim
Memorial Foundation 1977–78; Earthwatch Inc., Belmont, Massachusetts
1977; Northern Arts 1980–81; National Endowment for the Arts 1982.
He has exhibited widely in Britain and the USA. Publications include
Stonework of the Maya, University of New Mexico Press, Albuquerque
1974, *Mirrors and Windows*, Museum of Modern Art, New York 1978,
History of Photography in New Mexico, University of New Mexico Press
1978, *Monuments of the Incas* with text prepared by John Hemming, New
York Graphic Society 1982, *Architecture: Theory*, Lustrum Press, New
York, 1982. His work is in the collections of the Museum of Modern Art,
New York, Art Institute of Chicago, Princetown University Art
Museum, Victoria & Albert Museum, London, Amon Carter Museum,
Fort Worth, Texas, Polaroid Corporation, Cambridge, Massachusetts,
Seagrams Collection, New York.

The River Lune, from the Devil's Bridge, Kirkby, Lonsdale

Wastwater from Whin Rigg

Wastwater

Near Temple Sowerby

William Scammell

Lives in Cockermouth, and works as Staff Tutor in Literature (Cumbria) for Newcastle University's Department of Adult Education. Publications include *Yes & No*, Peterloo Poets 1979, *Time Past*, Treovis Press 1982, *A Second Life*, Peterloo Poets 1982, and *Adam's Dream*, (ed. with Rodney Pybus), Cumbria Literature 1981. He also reviews for the *Times Literary Supplement* and *London Magazine*.

Poem Beginning with 'Well'

Well they cut down the tall hedge
and burnt it at the field's ending.
What with green sap and driving rain
it wouldn't catch at first, so petrol
was brought in. A flame sailed
thirty feet tall, heating me up through
window glass, and the brash cracked cleanly
in the roar. A dozen cows, heads giant
dreamy sycamore seeds, came down
to bathe in the smoking ash. I knew
that cows were curious, but not that they
were connossieurs of red-hot pyres.
For one whole week they gathered in that place
shifting and bumping like fat rowing boats
tied to a pier, and scoffed the lot,
ash, charcoal, mud, gouging a giant lick
where tides of grass now topple under rain.

The Screes

The screes are speeding down at perfect pitch
before they tuck themselves in envelopes
Wastwater seals and never means to post.
Clouds snuffle by, fat bridesmaids choked with tears.

The screes are swarming up the cliff to lay
their case in heaven. The water's indigo.
A cormorant, wings unpacked, hung out to dry,
stands phoenix-fixed upon a rock. The screes

are drowning out upon the lake, face up.
It rains stops rains; somewhere a bark. The screes
are deep and thinking one emotion through

like Hegel's avalanche of counterpoint
prodding the Absolute to a day's turn.
Sheep press their starter-buttons all night long.

The Road

The road runs straight, like Hadrian's Wall
nearby. Out in the wind, between coast
and coast, high nomansland, spectacular
wide-lidded skies, the sun's eye
balancing on cars. What blows through
is placelessness, the mother-stuff
you couldn't live with. Immanence
is all to do again, whether the heel-stamp
of a Roman god, or mocking waves
from jiggly severed hands in lorry-cabs.

Bridge

Where the brimming river takes a breath
the old stone bridge proposes. Working girls
clap homewards from tall benches; mobster gulls
plane in and stall, bob down to threat

the racing currents. There a castle leans
to moss and postcards, history's mullioned tank;
a car squats useless on the river bank;
the town, as usual, turns its back. Some day it means

to listen to that music, where cut stone
absorbs the sounding glint of water, stirs
one patriarchal foot, consents to moan

a triple nothing in each hollow mouth
pure as a spavined tom. Hark to the spurs
of gender, ravelling the virgin's oath!

October

Honey for the eye.

Wind floods the valley,
great shoal of time
breaking summer's dam.

I drove my boots
up Mellbreak and Red Pike,
dragging my lungs like a dog.

Up on the top
you had to squat
or be budged

and punched out
over the edge.
A cloud like a whale

sailed suddenly over a peak
almost within hand's reach
then shredded as it went.

Down, down those hunched
and muscled shoulders, legs
aghast at the flung eye.

Oaks
brittle up
from seas of moss;

my mind's
a simple hod now,
heaving me home like stone.

Monday, Monday

The auctioneer's a diva. From his shed
Hi pinny ped! Hi pinny ped!

floats out in aria. One cow do blink,
the packed-in squares of Herdwicks pool their stink

while capped and gaitered shepherds, taking in
exotic species such as me, drink gin

and bitter in the all-day-open pubs
deploring this year's weather and the barmaids bubs.

Three hefty ladies in the barbers' chat
of death, disaster, Mrs Newbold's hat

and Tessa's canny wedding. Over in ANTIQUES
Miss Cooper dusts the Romneys, shoos her pekes

from off the Persians, glances up to see
the High Street ticking, and a ghostly eye

in POET'S CORNER, where old dummies leer
across the decades in their classic gear.

The bank is humming. Sealed off behind glass
the clerks munch paper, and the big Moustache

sits down to business. Where there's muck, there too's
the pinstrip and the polished shoes,

the furrowed brows of farmers, who will keep
and pasture prejudice, as they do sheep.

I'm just an idler; he's a narrow brute
whose mind is laced up in his boot . . .

But on the bridge, where placid Derwent slows
the racy stride of Cocker, we touch nose

at one another as we pass, sniff hard
respectively, the blank sheet and the knackers yard.

Faith Shannon

Born at Dehra Dun, India in 1928. She trained at Belfast College of Art, Central, Camberwell, London School of Printing, Goldsmiths, and Royal College of Art. She is now lecturer in charge of Bookbinding at Brighton Polytechnic and was awarded the M.B.E. for services to bookbinding in 1977. Recent exhibitions include *Designer Bookbinders*, Victoria & Albert Museum and USA tour 1972; *The Craftsman's Art*, Victoria & Albert Museum 1973; *Designer Bookbinders*, CAC Gallery, London and Centrode bel Libro, Ascona, Switzerland 1974; *Masterpiece*, British Crafts Centre, London 1977; *Handbookbinding Today*, San Francisco Museum of Modern Art 1978; *Paper & Ink*, British Crafts Centre 1978; *Work in Progress*, Crafts Council touring exhibition 1979; One person show, Ulster Museum, Belfast 1980; Parnham House 1981. Her work is held in private collections in Britain and abroad, and in Windsor Royal Library, British Museum, Victoria & Albert Museum, Crafts Council, Lilly Library, Indiana University, USA.

'The Very Rich Hours of Le Boulvé', Anthony Gross

Jon Silkin

Born in London in 1930 and educated at Wycliffe and Dulwich Colleges. He was awarded the Gregory Fellowship in Poetry at the University of Leeds in 1958, where he remained to take a degree in English and later to undertake original research on the poets of the First World War. In 1965 he moved to Newcastle, to continue editing, with a subsidy from Northern Arts, the magazine *Stand* which he had founded in 1952. Selected publications include *The Peaceable Kingdom*, Chatto 1954, *The Two Freedoms*, Chatto 1958, *The Re-Ordering of the Stones*, Chatto 1961, *Nature with Man*, Chatto 1965, *Amana Grass*, Wesleyan U.P. and Chatto 1971, *Out of Battle – Poets of the First World War*, Oxford University Press 1972, *The Principle of Water*, Carcanet 1974, *The Little Time-Keeper*, Carcanet and MidNAG & W. W. Norton 1976, *Penguin Book of First World War Poetry*, Penguin & Penguin/Viking 1979, *The Psalms with their Spoils*, Routledge & Kegan Paul 1980, *Selected Poems*, Routledge & Kegan Paul 1980. *Nature with Man* was awarded the Geoffrey Faber Memorial Prize, 1966.

(Untitled)

Small hills, among the fells, come apart from the large
where streams drop; the water-flowers
bloom at the edges, or in the shallows, together,
and are white. Whoever comes here, comes, glad, at least
and as they look, it is with some care, you can feel
that on flower, may tree, or dry-stone wall
their gaze collects in a moist, comely pressure.
I feel this, but slog elsewhere.
Swan Hunter's is where we build naval craft;
they emerge: destroyer, the submarine
fitted, at length, by electricians. Their work
is inspected; it is again re-wired. In the heat
men walk high in the hulk on planks, one
of them tips, and he falls the depth of the hold.
It is hot. The shithouses are clagged, the yard's
gates closed for security. The food is not good.
Some people in here are maimed.
I am trying to make again the feeling
plants have, and each creature has, looked at,
demure, exultant. The man who has fallen
looks at me, and looks away.

Strike

The earth comes moist-looking, and blackens;
a trickle of earth where the feet pressed,
twice a day, wearing off the grass.
Where the miners
were seen: a letter blown damply
into the corner of a hut: 'Oh dear love, come to me'
and nothing else.

Where are they?
The sheep bleat back to the mist balding
with terror; where
are they? The miners
are under the ground.

A pale blue patch of thick worsted
a scrag of cotton;
the wheel is still that washed the pounded ore.
They were cut down.

Almost turned by water, a stammer of the huge wheel
groping at the bearings.
Their bayonets; the red coat
gluey with red.

The water shrinks
to its source. The wheel,
in balance.

Spade

George Culley, Isaac Greener?

A want of sound hangs
in a drop of moisture from the wheel that
turned and washed the ore.

A rustling of clothes on the wind. The water does not move.

I have come here to be afraid.
I came for love to bundle
what was mine. I am scared
to sneak into the hut to find your coat.

When you put down your pick,
when other wouldn't sprag
the mine's passages; when you said no:

soldiers, who do not strike,
thrust
their bayonets into you.

They were told to.

The young mayor, shitting, closeted
with chain on his neck. I want to

push my hands into your blood
because I caused you to use yours.

I did not die; love, I did not. All the parts
of England fell melting like lead away,
as you showed me the melting once, when you and the men
with you were jabbed,

and without tenderness, were filled over;
no psalm, leaf-like, shading the eyelid
as the eye beneath is dazed abruptly
in the earth's flare of black light
burning after death.

The spade digging in the sunlight illuminates the face of my
                    God.

Blind him.

First to Last

1

The Milky Way: a chart, a conducting
of white bodies
lit by time in darkness. Off

in another place, spirals of milk
curd that darkness. If we fell
to where would we fall? Prodigal forms

that pour away.

There's no grasping them: no name
reveals the parent

in heavenly nakedness.

2

Here sprouts Meldon: *Moel-Dun*,
a hill
shimmered by cross, by cross or sign:

to house, to haven, in 1242

the needful light.

Church as a long room, chancel and nave
one plain intrication. Snug house

a round low vault of stars
ceilings in blue crosses, blood and blue,
shadowed with gold.

Were we gentle, so would this be.

3

Traumas of smoky shadow.

Bolam: of two names one
forced on the other: swollen ground.

Creation names her groin.

But before this, where we cut
their shades from us, place of the tree-trunks.

The likely pastures char.

Sheared from Rome, the Causeway
runs off. Poind and his stony dog
mark the foot's emigrations

grass persists in. Mound and stone

ponder the North's shadows:
the acreage of green farmers
under huge leaves annihilating
in shade their greenest powers.

Amongst the tumulus the short
dolerite coffin, grained with soot
upon the lumpy

glutinous flesh. I can't say.

For what's there, what is it? eyelid
bereft of coin, no bones
tumbling through earth. The grave

envelops no name. Death
has burnt away.

And smoke, lingering.

The Church is getting Short of Breath

Sabbath of the pensive spread buttocks.

Conscience, the size of a dried pea,
chafes over the pews flesh sweating

its Sabbath juice.

Douser of burning wax: old man
hugs remorse like a first wife. What labour
will such bridal pains be fruitful with?

First night of marriage wakes the bride
to shimmering kindness; our hemisphere
dishes the Sabbath, dead prayers,

the dulled rose of texts, desert mica.
Air breeds to the shy nibbling tourist.
Work-day fingers the rosary of work-days.

Work's necessary bead, – the mechanic
wrenches the thread by which our lives
fasten to us.

Coming first to church, sharp
as the warrior wren. Morning dews
the prompt mind, tourist of the holy
places pious with no use.

This is the true debating-ground,
and here the praying hands consume
the life they build. I shall do what I can.

The question loses its memory,
and the dense shade, in the spaces, runs
to hydrogen

laconic as its dull copulars.

Sneck the latch-door; Adam from sculpted
wood raises Eve with himself
to the bridal shapes. Love congregating

the bench will have its forked play
of their clasped forms: I have come to an end

of the ancient days. Laboured tweed
surplices the rich man.

My lovely parents, when you shaded
each in the other's thought, and flesh
pleaded one anatomy, of life,

endless life, death's frail nucleus
sweated to come alive, its soul
in our flesh. I loved my origins.

But you mid-wifed death. So I became
man, and as others judged me you
I judged. O gentle God, with both hands

you lathed prayer, a chariot's flange, God
of hope. The stars' system contracts,
that, or they flee us. Of such fountains

we lie in the solar ground, and the question
loses its mark.

Entropy at Hartburn

Between the hoof's cleft loam squeezes;
so beasts enter night-fall. Steamy
presences; the dunged breaths falter.

Hartburn divides night on itself
with a shutter. 'Mildred clamp out the dark.' Cream lace
embroiders its holes.

The huge energies untwine, and stars
slither away on the braids. The wagging stems
of sex slather to inane fruitfulness.

Not a thing to comfort us. The holly's fruit
taps at the church's stained glass
where solstice clenches its day,

and small energies out-thorn, the profusion
of winter at mid-night.

From 'The Little Time-keeper'

Melanie Sproat

Educated at High Wycombe College and at the Royal College of Art.
Awards include Johnson Matthey Metals Ltd., Silver Award 1975;
Licentiateship to Society of Designer Craftsmen, 1976; Northern Arts,
Craftsmanship 1978; Crafts Council, New Craftsmen Grant 1979.
She moved from London to Cumbria in 1978 to convert a disused
outbuilding at the Brewery Arts Centre into her workshop. She
specializes in contrasting the colour, structure and tactile qualities of
mixed metals, the purity and unique whiteness of silver offset against base
metals like copper, brass, nickel and steels. Further colour is added to the
surface by oxidization techniques using heat, chemicals or anodizing. She
exhibits mostly in London galleries, but has recently completed a touring
exhibition at venues in the North of England.

White metal box with outer jacket of oxidised cast bronze

Donald Wilkinson

Painter/printmaker, born Keswick in 1937. Has recently given up
teaching to return to Cumberland to set up an etching studio. He spends a
lot of time walking in and drawing the Cumbrian landscape.
His work is in many public collections including the Victoria & Albert
Museum, the Arts Council of Great Britain, the British Council, and
many Art Galleries. He has been a prize winner at the British Print
Biennales 1974–76, and the Cracow Print Biennale 1980.
Recent commissions include etchings for the
Wordsworth Museum, Grasmere.

Saddleback

Rydal Water, Winter

Derwentwater from Latrigg, Winter

July evening towards Causey Pike

Jonathan Williams

Poet, essayist, photographer, director of the Jargon Society, a literary foundation which has been publishing new British and American poets and photographers for some 30 years. He divides his year between a cottage in Dentdale, Cumbria and a farm in the Blue Ridge mountains near Highlands, North Carolina. His publications in 1981 included *The Fifty-two Clerihews of Clara Hughes*, a revised edition of *Blues & Roots/Rue & Bluets*, *Get Hot or Get Out*, Selected Poems, USA, and *Niches Inches*, Selected Poems, UK.

Six 'Elementals'
From Walks on the Howgill Fells

Homage to A. Wainwright

Calders

(the bare, high top
which local farmers
always call
cold arse)

Ecker Secker Beck

(where an old farmer
named *Hacker*
once held *acres*,
the language makes
a three-beat joke)

Bowderdale

(pronounced *Boother-dull* –
good reminder in case
you presume to pronounce
anything without knowing)

Great Dummacks

(Joseph Wright's
English Dialect Dictionary
sez *dummock* is
a pile of dung
in the parlance of
the 'Lanky Twang';
if so,
this is an odd thing to call
a Westmorland fell
661 metres tall)

The Leathgill Bridge

(according to my ear
surely *the* bridge
to Middle-Earth)

Carlingill

(Kerlingile (1220) Old Norse:
old woman ravine . . .
who was the old woman?
and who, for that matter, was
the hob of Hobdale?

Gleanings
from the Rev. Thomas Dunham Whitaker's
History of the Wapentake of Ewecross,
Together with a Final Invitation by Adam Sedgwick

(1) Eastwards:

many a
winsome
valley intervening . . .

(2) The Tourist

requires to be well shod
and amply provided
against the wonders of
Yorkshire meteorology

(3) A Descent is Now Made

by the dobbie-haunted
Yallas Gill
to Dent

(4) Dent:

property of
Thorphin:
Thorphin de Thoresby,
the son of Dolphin,
the son of Gospatries,
the son of Arkyl,
the son of Aykfrith . . .

(5) Ibby Peril:

the haunt
it is said
of a ghastly old witch

particularly anxious
to clutch
inebriates

(6) A Clever Lass in Dent Could Do Four Things:

she knows how to sing and knit,
and she knows how to carry the kit,
while she drives her kye to pasture . . .

(7) 'Warm Your Hearts

by gazing over
a noble cluster
of dales!'

David Wright

Poet, translator, and editor, has lived in Cumberland and Westmorland for the last 15 years. His collected poems, *To the Gods the Shades*, appeared in 1976, followed in 1980 by *Metrical Observations*, both published by Carcanet Press. He has published three travel books on Portugal, besides editing the *Penguin Book of English Romantic Verse*, Thomas de Quincey's *Recollections of the Lakes and the Lake Poets*, the *Selected Poems of Thomas Hardy*, and in 1981, *Selected Poems and Prose of Edward Thomas*. Scolar Press is soon to bring out the first volume of his massive documentary anthology of the Romantic Movement. He has translated *Beowulf* and is at present working on a new verse translation of Chaucer's *Canterbury Tales* for Oxford University Press.

Procession

Sober the overhead trees, and fields tilted
And framed by laborious walls on the framing hills,
No colour but a heavy green of August
Till the sun steps over a cloud, and light falls bare
On a pastoral lake and valley, where tourists
In their bright anoraks have come to stare.

Beyond the rectory, over the stone bridge,
The band assembles, cardigans and gleaming brass,
Waits by the teashop and nursery gardens;
A trombone has gone to the gents in the coach park.
Under the church tower, among those gaily
Shirted, I take my place, a sight-seer.

From its due angle the afternoon sunlight
Glances on us, the children in white and green,
The boys with rushes and the girls garlanded,
And on the gravemounds lies, autumnal almost.

The parishioners, in Sunday best, are ready
To move in procession. The Rush-bearing at Grasmere

Begins to parade toward the Rothay Hotel
Slowly; band, vicar, sidesmen, and choir,
With hesitant banners, the living, and the new-born
In perambulators gaudy with flowers.
Out of sight now, turning the corner, they'll return
A moment later, as they did last year.

What hymn is the band playing? They reappear,
The local dwellers followed by children,
Here and now, past to be contained together;
Like the plain water that stumbles below
The bridge I stand on, keeping the bed of the stream,
So altering that it seems never to alter.

Caleb Barnes

Set on rising ground above the village
Is a memorial seat inscribed 'Caleb
Barnes', with a date, four years before my time,
'Twenty-six years the village schoolmaster'.
It looks toward a lake and famous mountains,
Skiddaw and Blencathra and Helvellyn,
And yet the focus of its contemplation
Turns from them, fixes on a bog between
Bassenthwaite and invisible Derwentwater:
A dingy morass, dyke-divided, whose
Dead paths and secret bridges Caleb Barnes
Only knew, and which now only I know,
Or so I think, because no one goes there:
Nothing to see but reedgrass; a mangrove
Copse of birdcherry, hornbeam, sunk in moss;
A few drowned fences of oxidized wire.
Because we loved the same neglected place
I feel I know the man I never met,
Although what drew him does not much draw me
Except as an occasional spectacle:
Orchids and water plants and waterfowl,
And, nameless to me, migrant winter birds.
All these he could, and did, identify,
A collector of life, of knowledge too;
Here he was happy and outside himself.
This is all I know about the man, except
The nondescript and untraversable flats
In different lights of winter, summer, spring,
And autumn, that shift round a bowl of hills
In clear or muffled weather; the altering
Colours of these four seasons that they wear;
I may suppose they meant as much to him.

The Two Streams

Pow Beck winds through our valley, parallel
With Newlands Beck, a faster lucid water.
It is a puzzle that they do not meet
Where they run side by side; or rather where
The one easily hastens, glancing by
The small stones of its bed, shallow and clear,
Almost as rapid as the skimming bird,
A white-waistcoated dipper that haunts it;
While the other meditates, hardly moves,
Luxurious under weed that hides its movement.
Here less than half a field divides the pair.
Later, beyond the concave of our valley,
The direct Newlands hurries to its aim,
And Pow hives off, ambles by Portinscale
Towards the moss, where fields lose coherence,
Eroded by marsh grasses: fences half
Sunk in the bogland, pastures abandoned
To various waterfowl. The characters
Of the two streams survive their change of ground.
Newlands, pursuing a successful course,
Gathers all mountain tributaries; Pow
Flows doubtfully, dossing by a thorn
And holly thicket where, in late July,
The cattle also drowse, and, year by year,
Two swans with their grey cygnets pluck the stream.
Pow, at the last, where reeds grow more thick,
Joins and dissolves in Newlands; which, now swollen,
Travels the slowlier, and further on
Broadens into the waters of a lake.

Balloon

To Max and Jane

We took the children on the lake.

Wings like heartbeats, a stretched neck
Skimming over hazy water
Between an island and an island:
A wildfowl flying, black with distance.

Then a balloon, another bounty,
Hung with slung basket low above
A wooded bight, a stony bay,
Drifted like an hour hand
Across the flat and sunlit face
Of the lake, both motionless.

Yes, they will remember this;
And as I did, when young as they,
Think what is given us to see
Has always been, will always be;
Heretofore as hereafter
A duck flying, a balloon
Suspended with two people in
Its basket over Derwentwater.

Mirehouse

The mountain's rooted in a lake.
Young and hypochondriac
Tennyson sent wheeling over
Its black-velvet, moonstruck water
An Excalibur, as he
Recapitulated Malory
In blank and plangent verse
While he stayed at Mirehouse.
The bamboo chair in which he sat
Sits in the library yet;
And comfortable windows stare
Georgian, reticent, severe,
At hills not high, but full of sheep,
And stable as a stable clock.
Below them, where lake water laps
Pebbles and the boles of oaks,
I see a woman read aloud
In sunlight, underneath green boughs,
And a boat float slowly by
The wooded point of a small bay,
With spread oars rested on rowlocks;
To the blade-rims cling water-drops.
Along the shore, on a cropped bent,
The chapel of an Irish saint
Raises its verticals, completes
The archaic picturesque.
Here a so civil wilderness
Of mere and mountain, moor and moss,
At autumn pricks against the sky
The wild geese as they fly away
In formal pattern overhead,
A wavering arrowhead.

Lake Scene

Built on conveyor belts,
They move along conveyor belts of tarmac.
Machines that graze on
Mountain, wood, and lake,
Pasture and ploughland, even

Homes and houses of men, and
The cities where they've come from.
Bobbles of painted metal,
Volvo, Ford, Rover, Datsun
– Silica gleam of locust-swarm –

Flip by a leafshaped lake
As good as any colour transparency;
Soft romantic mountains, framed
In a thousand windscreens daily,
And places like this, seen to death;

Or stop – and out come folding
Tables, chairs; plastic thermos;
Cups, plates, polythene cake,
Dog on leash, portable telly.
Awed, lakes and hills retreat.

Acknowledgements

We acknowledge with thanks permission to reprint the following works:
Fleur Adcock: *Binoculars*; *Going out from Ambleside*; (from Below
Loughrigg, Bloodaxe Books); *Maryport*; (Poetry Wales). Melvyn Bragg:
Cumbria (from The Illustrated London News). Thomas A. Clark:
Cat Leap Fall (from Ways Through Bracken, The Jargon Society).
Roger Garfitt: *Gardening in Avernus* (from New Poems 1976–77,
P.E.N. Anthology); *Buzzard Soaring* (from Aquarius); *The Broken Road*
(from Wall, L.Y.C. Press). Frances Horovitz: *Finding a Sheep's Skull*
(from Poetry Review); *For Stephen Procter* (from Writing Women).
Thomas Meyer: *Calends* (from Aggie Westons). Norman Nicholson:
To the River Duddon; (from Selected Poems, Faber & Faber); *The Black
Guillemot*; *Bee Orchid at Hodbarrow*; (from A Local Habitation, Faber &
Faber); *Scafell Pike*; *Cloud on Black Combe*; *Wall*; (from Sea to the West,
Faber & Faber). Rodney Pybus: *A Durable Music*; (from Wall, L.Y.C.
Press); *Almanac of Herons*; *Elterwater* (from Stand); *Not only Forms*;
Year of the White Horse; (from Stand BBC Radio 3). William Scammell:
Monday, Monday; *The Road*; (from Poetry Review); *The Screes*; (from
The Listener). Jon Silkin: *Untitled*; *Strike*; *Spade*; *Entropy at Hartburn*;
First to Last; *The Church is Getting Short of Breath*; (from Selected Poems,
Routledge and Kegan Paul). David Wright: *The Two Streams*; *Caleb
Barnes*; (from Metrical Observations, Carcanet Press); *Procession*; (from
To the Gods the Shades, Carcanet Press); *Mirehouse*; *Lake Scene*; *Balloon*;
(from A View of the North, Carcanet Press).
We acknowledge with thanks permission to print the following
photographers' work:
Prudence Cumming; Richard Davies (courtesy of Crafts magazine);
Ian Dobbie; Richard Padwick; Guy Pawle; Mark Prior.